Praise for *Leaders Leap*

"*Leaders Leap* by Steve Dennis stands as a beacon for modern business leadership. As the renowned author of *Remarkable Retail*, Steve once again demonstrates his deep understanding of the landscape in this compelling read. Steve's philosophy, deeply rooted in customer-centric values and the necessity to adapt to ongoing disruption, is more than just theory; it's a practical guide for today's leaders. This book brilliantly navigates the crossroads where tradition meets innovation, urging leaders to make bold choices. In a world where the only options are to be remarkable or become irrelevant, *Leaders Leap* is an essential road map for those ready to embrace transformation and lead with courage and vision."
–HAL LAWTON, president and CEO of Tractor Supply Company

"Steve Dennis is an evangelist for bold, radical transformation. Drawing on his extensive experience as both an executive and an advisor to leaders, he makes a persuasive case for urgency and fearlessness in pursuit of innovation. He shows how important it is to invest in our personal transformation—to identify and work on the things that hold us back from taking the bold, decisive, meaningful actions that will save our businesses from drifting toward irrelevance. Any leader seeking a remarkable future will benefit from adopting all seven mind leaps described in this entertaining book."
–SALLY ELLIOTT, partner and co-leader of the Global Retail Practice, Spencer Stuart

"*Leaders Leap* is a timely examination of the pitfalls leaders encounter during business transformations. Going beyond strategy, Steve Dennis pinpoints how ego, vulnerability, ignorance, and fear hinder bold action and rapid progress. Updating classic business concepts for the digital age, this book offers a concise road map for success amidst our current age of disruption. It's a must-read for leaders looking to transform their companies and leap into the future."
–HUBERT JOLY, former CEO of Best Buy, senior lecturer at Harvard Business School, and author of *The Heart of Business*

"At a time when virtually every part of our economy is being reshaped by the forces of disruption, Steve Dennis makes the case that 'safe is risky.' To rise above the rest, transformational leadership requires a greater focus on boldness. We need to aim higher in the value we deliver and move much faster. *Leaders Leap* is your indispensable guide to a more remarkable future for you and your organization."
–MINDY GROSSMAN, partner at Consello Group and former CEO of WW International

"This book reminds us that transformation is not driven by technology but by courageous leaders who see reality and then adapt themselves and their companies to leap ahead of others. In an AI age, it will be HI, or Human Inspiration, that will set companies and leaders apart. The ability to see what others cannot, create solutions that are both simple and impactful, and to do so in ways that both move fast and move others. Read this book to turbocharge yourself and your business."
–**RISHAD TOBACCOWALLA,** senior advisor at Publicis Groupe and author of *Restoring the Soul of Business*

"We all bring critical thinking and strong business practices to the work that we do. We identify clear opportunities and challenges and work toward solving them efficiently, reliably, and with rigor. Steve Dennis's latest book, *Leaders Leap*, is an acute reminder that in a time of technological shifts and dances, leaders need to add emergent thinking into the mix. *Leaders Leap* gives you permission to generate better ideas, push innovation, explore new opportunities, and even improvise to get there. How radical can you be? Read on and find out."
–**MITCH JOEL,** cofounder of ThinkersOne and author of *Six Pixels of Separation* and *Ctrl Alt Delete*

"Future-proofing our organizations demands we go beyond the latest conceptual frameworks and adoption of new processes. We must adopt fundamentally new mindsets. In this ground-breaking book, Steve Dennis presents a paradigm shift that calls on leaders to seek higher ground, act more boldly, and move much faster if they hope to survive, much less thrive."
–**TIFFANI BOVA,** bestselling author of *The Experience Mindset*, executive advisor, and three-time Thinkers50

LEADERS LEAP

Transforming Your Company at the Speed of Disruption

STEVE DENNIS

WONDERWELL

Library of Congress Control Number: 2023914618

ISBN 978-1-63756-029-7 (hardcover)
ISBN 978-1-63756-030-3 (EPUB)

Editor: Adam Rosen
Cover design and interior design: Adrian Morgan
Cover image: iStockphoto
Author photograph: Chris West, Video Narrative

Published by Wonderwell in Los Angeles, CA
www.wonderwell.press

WONDERWELL

Printed and bound in Canada

To Elena and Claire,
for everything, but mostly
the love and the laughter.

To Seth, who encouraged me to leap
before I believed I was ready and
supported me unconditionally
once I discovered I was.

And to all those, known and unknown,
who stand at the precipice
and bravely dare to leap.

I will not follow where the path may lead, but I will go where there is no path, and I will leave a trail.

—MURIEL STRODE

Here's to the crazy ones. The misfits. The rebels. The troublemakers. The round pegs in the square holes. The ones who see things differently. They're not fond of rules, and they have no respect for the status quo.

—APPLE'S "THINK DIFFERENT" TV COMMERCIAL

CONTENTS

Introduction: Mind the Gap   1

PART 1   Remarkable or Irrelevant?   21

Chapter 1 Shift Happens   23
Chapter 2 The Curse of the Timid Transformation   43

PART 2   The Seven Leadership Mind Leaps   57

Chapter 3 Mind Leap 1: Crush Your Ego   59
Chapter 4 Mind Leap 2: Wake Up   77
Chapter 5 Mind Leap 3: Special, Not Big   93
Chapter 6 Mind Leap 4: Start with Wow   113
Chapter 7 Mind Leap 5: Think Radically   127
Chapter 8 Mind Leap 6: Safe Is Risky   145
Chapter 9 Mind Leap 7: Faster, Faster, Go, Go, Go!   161

PART 3   Leaders Leap   177

Chapter 10 The Big Leap   179

Acknowledgments   193
Notes   197
Selected Bibliography and Additional Reading   205
About the Author   209
Also by Steve Dennis   211

INTRODUCTION
MIND THE GAP

If you don't like change,
you're going to like irrelevance even less.

—ERIC SHINSEKI, retired United States Army general

IT'S A CRISP FALL DAY IN 2002, and I'm enjoying my second cup of coffee in my office at Sears's sprawling corporate campus outside of Chicago. The last eighteen months have been exhausting for me and my team, but on this particular morning, I'm feeling pretty good.

The previous afternoon we had presented our long-term transformation plan to the Sears board of directors. Our recommendations were thorough and expansive, but we knew we might face resistance. Putting our plans into action would require billions of dollars in investment and many complicated and painful changes. If successful—and there were hardly any guarantees—it would take years to fully realize the benefits. To move from design and testing into comprehensive action, we needed the board's full-throated assent.

We got it.

They were ready, they said, to do what had to be done. They would invest real money to recapture Sears's promise and reboot the storied retailer, positioning it for a better future.

From a personal perspective, this felt like a huge achievement. The previous year, I had been promoted to vice president of corporate strategy and joined the company's senior leadership team. I had several responsibilities, but by far the most important and vexing one was helping craft a turnaround strategy for Sears's long-suffering department store business. Although Sears had once been the biggest, most valuable retailer on the planet (as you probably know), for more than a decade the company's retail market share, competitive situation, and financial performance had declined dramatically.

The blows were coming from all sides—and had been for many years. Discount mass merchants like Walmart, Target, and Kohl's were stealing away more value- and convenience-oriented customers. So-called category killers like Home Depot and Lowe's in home improvement and Best Buy in appliances and consumer electronics had become formidable, rapidly expanding competitors. They were starting to erode Sears's once overwhelmingly dominant (and highly profitable) market position. Our situation was growing increasingly dire.

This wasn't Sears's first attempt at a turnaround. Far from it. Multiple past leadership regimes had tried to return Sears to its glory days. They'd done some innovative things, including launching the high-profile "Softer Side of Sears" campaign in the mid-1990s and following that quickly with an early and quite substantial investment in e-commerce. Numerous specialty concepts that were not tethered to regional mall real estate had been piloted and expanded to varying degrees of success. Still, none were stemming what increasingly looked like a potential slow slide into oblivion for what was the first and, at the time, most famous "everything store."

In late 2000, Alan Lacy was named Sears's new CEO. He moved quickly to assemble a new leadership team, eventually appointing me to head up corporate strategy. Once again it was time to mount an attempt at a bold turnaround.

So we dug into customer data and conducted extensive competitive analysis. With the assistance of a prominent strategy consulting firm, we executed many rounds of consumer research to understand what was most critical to the customers we desperately needed to win, grow, and retain.

As we got further into the process and learned much more about our opportunities and weaknesses, we began piloting multiple tracks across the company to experiment with new strategies. We consolidated and developed new private brands, created new marketing campaigns, and explored a comprehensive redesign of our store operating model, layout, and visual merchandising. All were aimed at dramatically improving customer relevance and driving greater profitability. We were onto something big—or so we thought.

It wasn't all analysis and experimentation. A few months before we presented our longer-term vision, we'd written a check for nearly $2 billion to acquire Lands' End, with the aim of enhancing our apparel and home businesses and accelerating our growing e-commerce and direct-to-consumer capabilities. A new big-box, "off-the-mall" concept called Sears Grand was being designed completely from the ground up and would open the next year.

It was an ambitious agenda, and my team had played an indispensable role. And now we had the board's support to scale up our experiments and roll out the complete turnaround strategy. We'd done just about everything we'd originally set out to accomplish when I started in my new position. Having worked in strategy and innovation for the better part of my career, I know that pitching such an ambitious plan is not usually so successful, no matter how necessary one's efforts might be.

But back to that fateful fall day. As I sat at my conference table basking in our success, I was suddenly jolted out of my self-congratulatory daydream when one of my direct reports poked his head into my office. John had played an essential role in the competitive and customer analysis, and he was also helping lead the development of our new concept store. He looked dismayed.

"What's up?" I queried.

"I've been reflecting on the strategy we came up with," he began. "I definitely think it really is the best we can do given the circumstances. But the more I think about it, it isn't really a strategy to win. It's just a strategy to suck less."

I was perplexed. What was he talking about? Did he not remember all the fantastic work we had just completed? Did he not appreciate how hard it was to get the executive team's alignment and ultimately secure the board's support? *We'd nailed this thing.* We were going to be the saviors of Sears.

But then—slowly at first, and then all at once—a sinking feeling started to consume me.

Questions I had repressed or denied began to fill my head. Even if everything we had planned was flawlessly executed, were our actions really bold enough to meaningfully differentiate ourselves from our competition? Could we possibly move fast enough to close the gap that had developed and widened because of our slowness to act for so very many years?

Fundamentally, were we actually leaping to a new leadership position or essentially running to stand still?

My veil of denial began to part.

Shit.

John was right.

MIND THE GAP

Fast-forward to late 2022, some twenty years later. I'm about to go onstage in front of an audience of nearly one thousand retail executives in a windowless ballroom at an expansive and quite luxurious Florida resort.

I'm the annual conference's main keynote speaker, and I've been hired to share my thoughts about the current state of retail, where I see the industry heading, and how companies need to respond. I'm armed with nearly ninety PowerPoint slides, and I've got forty minutes to drop some serious wisdom.

I've given iterations of this presentation—which largely draws on key themes from my first book, *Remarkable Retail: How to Win and Keep Customers in the Age of Disruption*—many dozens of times, on stages big and small, across six continents. My experience at Sears all those years ago, my subsequent role as a senior executive at Neiman Marcus, and more recently my work advising dozens of organizations as a strategy and innovation consultant have all greatly informed the creation and refining of my core points.

Shortly before I'm due onstage, however, I call an audible. I decide to mix up my usual opening even though I didn't have any corresponding visuals, nor any time to rehearse it. Most professional speakers will tell you that this is a terrible idea. For good reason.

Yet sitting in my hotel room earlier that morning prepping for my appearance, I suddenly felt compelled to embrace a different approach. I was confident that my talk was well crafted—and I certainly was well prepared to deliver the goods onstage just a few hours later. But I had a growing and gnawing sense that perhaps my message needed to be more direct, more provocative, more urgent. Maybe it's because I decided it was time to take my own advice and shift my mindset. Go out on a limb. Make a leap. Aim to be more remarkable.

So after a fair amount of time nervously pacing around my room and playing out various scenarios in my head, I began scribbling some idea fragments in my notebook. Here's a cleaned-up version of what I remember jotting down that day:

- Profound, often seismic shifts continue to ripple through all industries, upending just about every aspect of what customers want, what defines competitive advantage, and what leads to long-term success.

- In a world of abundant choice and increasingly frictionless 24/7 access, even very good is no longer good enough. Anything less than remarkable risks being ignored. To command customers' attention, earn their business, and cement their loyalty, we have to amplify the wow—that is, create far greater distance between what we deliver and what the competition offers.

- The pace of disruption continues to accelerate, frequently becoming far more exponential than linear.

- Increasingly, what companies call innovation or transformation is not close to being bold enough, nor is it being implemented quickly enough, to keep pace with where customers, leading-edge technology, and best-in-class competition is today and will be headed in the future.

- Unless companies become aware of the widening disconnect between what is needed and what they are doing, truly accept this growing and powerful reality, and take aggressive action, they are likely doomed to irrelevance—or even worse, complete extinction.

- For many organizations, taking action requires more than merely working harder at existing business optimization programs or even what they currently consider transformation initiatives. It requires a complete reset. A comprehensive reboot. A leap to a wholly new paradigm.

- This new reality creates an ever-widening gap—a transformation gap.

The last insight struck me as the most essential one and a distillation of all the others. Further inspired, I grabbed another piece of paper and sketched out a simple chart to illustrate this gap. Here's the subsequent professionally rendered version of it.

—— THE TRANSFORMATION GAP ——

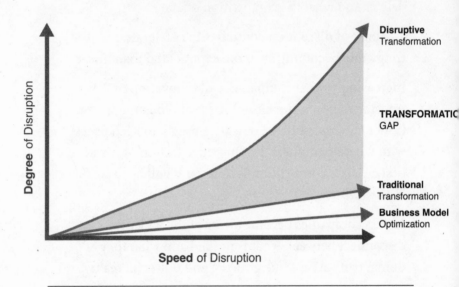

I decided to run with it.[1]

Just minutes into my talk, despite having to comically pantomime my hastily created chart concept, I could tell by the rapt attention and uncomfortable shifting in seats that I had struck a nerve with many members of the audience.

When I stated that this gap would only grow wider for most companies given their slow-and-steady trajectory, I saw a lot of heads nodding.

When I opined that organizations' failure to aim much higher with competitive differentiation and to move far faster to close this gap would, over time, risk irrelevance—and perhaps even put many organizations out of business—knowing murmurs filled the vast conference hall.

Well, now that I've got your attention . . .

At that point I somewhat clumsily segued back to my original presentation, which covered the essential actions organizations needed to take to get on a more remarkable path to the future. That is, the actions they must take to have any future at all.

As I concluded my keynote and left the stage, dozens of attendees sprinted up to the front of the room to talk with me. They shared that they were worried that the organizations they worked for—or with—weren't changing nearly quickly enough. They were concerned that too much of what consumed leadership's attention was far too incremental and mostly aimed at defending the status quo. Many said they were very concerned that their organizations were fundamentally and irreversibly stuck.

Maybe I was onto something?

INNOVATE OR DIE

When I left Sears about a year after our seemingly successful board presentation, I knew that things would end badly for the iconic retailer. Our new strategy made us better, but it didn't come close to making us remarkable in a world that was changing faster and faster. There was no leap to an exciting future, just actions to try and plug an increasingly leaky bucket.

To paraphrase one of my former bosses after he had also departed: "We all know how this movie ends. We just don't know how many minutes are left."

If only past regimes had not been blinded by hubris. If only they had paid more attention to what was really going on with shifts in consumer preferences, the impact of technology, and new competitive dynamics. If only they'd been more willing to take greater risks and compete with themselves. If only they had been willing to change more radically. If only they had started earlier and moved much faster, perhaps a precipitous dive could have been averted. If only, if only, if only.

Of course, we'll never know for sure. But even though the Sears story is among the more extreme examples of companies who have lost their way, it is not unique to retail.

The once very mighty have fallen across a spectrum of industries. Kodak and Polaroid. Compaq, BlackBerry, Gateway, and Palm (creator of the Palm Pilot). Oldsmobile, Pontiac, and Saturn. Pan Am. Myspace. As well as RadioShack, Pier 1, and many more. The list is a long one and continues to grow.

At the same time, plenty of big companies have managed to get unstuck in the face of relentless disruption. Or, better yet, have refused to put themselves in a position to get stuck in the first place.

Perhaps my favorite example is Netflix, which in its relatively short life span has fundamentally reinvented itself twice. This story arc is brilliantly summarized by a billboard the company posted in Hollywood back in 2021.

As every CEO understands (or should), customer preferences are increasingly being reshaped by an ever-shifting mix of competitive offerings. The rapid growth of e-commerce and social media presents customers with new ways to gather information about products and pricing. Advances in digital technology make things possible right now (or in the very near future) that could barely be imagined a few years ago. Powerful new competitors are emerging seemingly every day.

The reasons that iconic, once-vibrant brands fail are varied and in some cases complex. But an argument could also be made that because they existed and thrived long before digital disruption became a force, they had plenty of time to address the problems that led to their demise. The organizations that are struggling to survive today—or those that will soon find themselves gasping for air—have no such luxury.

Customers are demanding more. Insurgent competitors are raising the bar ever higher on what drives market share, customer loyalty, and financial results. Technology continues to reshape the landscape. So, to hesitate or to merely focus on incremental change is to risk falling farther and farther behind.

And once the gap widens between what customers demand and what we can deliver, catching up to the competition that aimed higher, acted more boldly, moved much faster—in other words, that leaped across that chasm—will not just be difficult. It may very well be impossible.

BUILT TO FAIL

It's not like most organizations don't know this. Studies consistently make it clear that most executives are worried about disruption and how ill prepared they are to effectively deal with it. If you picked up this book, chances are you feel the same way. The problem—the gigantic issue looming like an asteroid about to strike—is either that they aren't doing anything about it, or if they are, their efforts will most likely fall well short of what's needed.

Here's what I mean. In a 2021 study, McKinsey & Company found that over 80 percent of executives report that innovation is among their organization's top three priorities. Yet less than 10 percent say they are satisfied with their company's innovation performance.[2]

In its 2023 Disruption Index study, AlixPartners found that 78 percent of the CEOs surveyed indicated that their companies faced serious disruption in the past year (up 10 percent from the year earlier).[3] Moreover, they highlighted many concerning findings, including:

- **98 percent say their business model must change in the next three years, but 85 percent say they find it hard to know where to start.**

- **75 percent worry their organizations are not adapting fast enough, and 72 percent say their executive teams lack sufficient agility.**

- **65 percent say technology is changing at a rate they can't keep up with.**

- **70 percent are worried about losing their jobs.**

It's worth asking the question: Why is everyone so anxious and unsure?

After all, disruption isn't new. It's not hard to find books, white papers, podcasts, TED talks, and the like that stress the importance of innovation and lay out the process changes necessary to respond to these inexorable forces.

Many (if not most) organizations include "innovation" in their mission statements and investor presentations. In the last few years, it's become commonplace for CEOs to talk about how their company is undertaking a transformation strategy or is committed to transforming. Many have even created a new role in their C-suite: chief transformation officer.

And yet almost always the result is at best incremental change and at worst lots of flailing that sets the company on a path to more and more struggle and perhaps even an extinction event. In fact, another McKinsey study from 2021 found that 70 percent of transformations fail.[4]

I'd wager that this statistic isn't very shocking to you. If you've been in the workforce for a decent amount of time, there's a good chance you've experienced—or maybe had a hand in—this painful process.

To me, this is a clear sign that the current advice for disruption-proofing your future isn't cutting it. There must be a way to get off a road to nowhere. In the chapters that follow, that's what I aim to help you do.

THE INNOVATOR'S (NEW) DILEMMA

This book does not plow entirely new ground. The late, great Clayton M. Christensen explored similar territory in 1997 with his groundbreaking book *The Innovator's Dilemma: When New Technologies Cause Great Firms to Fail,* and his 2003 follow-up (with Michael E. Raynor), *The Innovator's Solution: Creating and Sustaining Successful Growth.*

Christensen, who coined the term *disruptive innovation,* observed that large, successful companies were at risk of being made obsolete by new technologies brought to market by industry outsiders (or far smaller companies).

In the process of describing the problem, he made the

critical distinction between "sustaining technologies" (namely, those that seek to optimize performance along established dimensions of customer value) and "disruptive technologies" (i.e., those that fundamentally alter the competitive landscape of an existing industry or lead to an entirely new competitive sector).

Said differently, sustaining technology helps you do what you already do, but better. Truly disruptive technology, on the other hand, solves a problem in an entirely new way and/or attracts a wholly new set of customers by reimagining the value equation.

As an example, technology that allows a taxi driver to take a customer payment faster or cheaper is sustaining. The technology that enabled the creation of Uber and Lyft is disruptive.

Christensen goes on to explain that among the reasons why industry incumbents often fail to react adequately to disruptive threats is that they are overly focused on preserving and optimizing their existing core business (i.e., leveraging what they already do). He points the finger directly at these leaders, arguing that their tendency to stick with what has previously determined their success gets in the way of seeing the next—or an entirely different—mountain that must be scaled.

In other words: they do everything Sears had been doing for quite some time.

———————

The reason [why great companies failed] is that good management itself was the root cause. Managers played the game the way it's supposed to be played. The very decision-making and resource allocation processes that are key to the success of established companies are the very processes that reject disruptive technologies: listening to customers; tracking competitors' actions carefully; and investing resources to design and build higher-performance, higher-quality products that will yield greater profit.[5]

—CLAYTON CHRISTENSEN
THE INNOVATOR'S DILEMMA

———————

As I will unpack in the upcoming chapters, much of what Christensen argued in *The Innovator's Dilemma* is still very much in force today.

But much has changed as well. Customer wants and needs have evolved in ways that Christensen could not have envisioned in the late '90s and early 2000s. The technologies that are truly disruptive now and that will reshape the competitive landscape in the future were primitive iterations or on only a few people's radar when his work first started to have impact. Social and economic forces are playing out in wholly new ways, propelled by a vast web of connection, adoption of game-changing technologies, radically increased processing speed, lowered data storage costs, and much, much more.

Although Christensen correctly focused primarily on the changes individual managers need to address to resolve this critical dilemma—largely steering clear of many of his contemporaries' tendencies to talk in more abstract terms about the "organization," "culture," or "the firm"—his core advice still sits firmly in the domain of strategic management theory.

Given all the tectonic shifts of the past two decades, in my view this is a highly necessary starting point, but one that is far from sufficient.

Yes, remarkable leadership requires a deep understanding of these important management principles and corporate strategy theories. But future-proofing our organizations must go beyond the latest conceptual frameworks and adoption of new processes. We must also adopt fundamentally new mindsets.

It remains true that strategic misunderstanding and fierce protection of legacy practices have a huge role in hindering vital progress. But there are just as many, for lack of a better term, psychological or emotional barriers that leaders must overcome if they are to thoroughly transform for a new era and do so at the speed of disruption. Within the past decade, a whole new set of challenges have emerged that require much more than strategic thinking to overcome. These challenges require entirely *new* ways of thinking.

LEADERS LEAP

There are plenty of excellent books specifically detailing how one should go about improving their innovation processes. This won't be one of them.

Successful transformation isn't simply about finding a better cookbook than the one you already have. It's about embracing wholly new ways of thinking and acting—what I call *mind leaps*—to guide you on what can be a perilous journey. And here I very much mean you as a leader, not some abstraction of your company, organization, culture, or brand.

I believe we need to accept a new paradigm, one which requires us to blow up much of what we've done in the past and rethink many of our long-held leadership principles. Stated simply, we're doing it wrong.

Business optimization and what counts as a transformation program at most companies, even if spectacularly well executed, are perfectly sound concepts. But they are very unlikely to lead to the degree of substantial, differentiated, sustainable competitive advantage needed to survive, much less thrive, in the future. Moreover, the pace at which most of these strategies are being operationalized is far too slow to keep pace with the speed of disruption.

Our aim has to be much, much higher. And we must move much, much faster. We have to leap.

UP AND TO THE RIGHT

Aim Higher

LEAP TO THE FUTURE

Degree of Disruption

Move Faster

Speed of Disruption

Today, tomorrow, and for the foreseeable future.

In **Part One**, I will describe in deeper detail the emerging, uncomfortable realities that organizations and the leaders who run them face. I will also analyze the growing—and increasingly dangerous—gap between what is needed and what is being done, and why attempts to close this gap are usually far too timid considering what's at stake.

Part Two offers solutions to the problems spelled out in Part One. These solutions take the form of seven fundamental mind leaps leaders need to make to navigate disruption's churning waters. Leaders who embrace them will be far better prepared to help their organizations close the gap and thrive well into the future.

That's the good news. The tougher medicine is that such a rigorously honest examination of how our ego defects, blind spots, confirmation biases, defense mechanisms, ardent desires, and deepest fears get in the way of the progress we need to make can be very uncomfortable and, at times, quite unsettling. But that doesn't negate its essential importance. Sometimes the truth hurts.

In **Part Three**, I'll close with my advice for incorporating these mind leaps into your organizational practice, building a sustainable transformation engine, and further developing the skills you need to surf the inevitable waves of disruption we all encounter.

Along the way I will infuse this book with my own varied and illustrative experiences as a C-suite leader at two Fortune 500 companies, a strategic advisor to, and board member of, numerous for-profit and nonprofit organizations, an executive leadership coach, and someone who has dissected business strategies for nearly forty years. I will share warnings and stories of things I wish knew back then or wish I had better appreciated during the course of my journey. Let's just say, mistakes were made.

My intention is to help you recognize that it *is* possible to transform radically even with disruption nipping at your heels—or chomping on your torso. That you can win the epic battle between being remarkable or becoming irrelevant. But before you do any of this, you must change yourself.

Leaders leap.

PART 1

REMARKABLE OR IRRELEVANT?

CHAPTER 1

SHIFT HAPPENS

If you're not nervous,
you're not paying attention.

—MILES DAVIS

I **GREW UP IN THE OUTLYING SUBURBS OF NEW YORK CITY** in the 1960s and '70s. Like other middle-class kids from the area, I spent many a weekend being dragged around by my mother to go shopping at stores like Abraham & Strauss, Caldor, and Bamberger's.

On family road trips we often stopped at Howard Johnson's for lunch or a snack.

As I got older, Lord & Taylor became my go-to place to buy my nana a birthday or Christmas present.

In college, my favorite places to buy albums (whether vinyl or 8-track) were Tower Records and Sam Goody.

After I got my MBA, I worked for a large global consulting firm and frequently lugged around a 22-pound Compaq computer on more plane trips than I care to mention.

Our firm's client reports were produced by an in-house graphics department that used a dedicated machine to take text from a Wang word processing workstation (that could only be operated by a trained administrative assistant) and Lotus 1-2-3 spreadsheets (printed out on a dot matrix printer) to turn them into good-looking hard-copy reports and "transparencies."

My first house was outfitted with furniture my then-wife and I had purchased from Marshall Field's and Carson Pirie Scott & Co.—two iconic Chicago department stores founded in 1852 and 1854, respectively.

For years, our bookcases were chockablock with a truly frightening number of CDs and VHS tapes.

As our young daughters grew older, a typical Friday night might include a trip to Blockbuster to rent a movie. Or maybe one of my kids would occupy herself playing a Game Boy.

Our first home computer came from Gateway. We accessed the internet by inserting an AOL floppy disk and connecting to the internet via a dial-up modem ("You've got mail!").

When I joined the senior leadership team at Neiman Marcus in 2004, much of my life seemed centered on my shiny new Palm Pilot. My colleagues were similarly glued to their devices—but, for whatever reason, theirs were primarily BlackBerrys.

You can probably see where I'm going with this.

Products, technologies, and brands that were once hugely popular in the not-too-distant past are now completely gone or mere shells of their former dominant selves.

Depending upon your age and where you live, your list may be a bit different, but that doesn't detract from the underlying point. The failure of organizations to be keenly aware of major shifts that are unfolding, accept them as an emerging reality, and take bold and decisive action armed with that knowledge creates a very real risk of fading into abject irrelevance. And it's happening faster and faster all the time.

SET THE WAYBACK MACHINE FOR 1995

Readers of a certain age will remember what shopping for just about anything was like toward the end of the last century, when the internet, for all intents and purposes, didn't exist.

Except for the small share of spending accounted for by mail-order catalogs, virtually all retail activity involved going to a physical location to see what the store had on sale, determining whether it fit your needs, toting your merchandise to a cash register, paying for it, and carting it home with you.

You had to hope the shops you visited had the particular model, size, style, or color you wanted in stock. For the most part, there was no way of knowing without investing time to go around to many different locations, each with different (and often limited) hours.

Gathering information about which products you might consider could also be time-consuming and not all that reliable. You tended to learn about products through the brand owner's advertising and/or from talking to salespeople— information that was neither comprehensive nor unbiased. If you were lucky, maybe a neighbor, family member, friend, or coworker had some experience with the product you were interested in, or maybe the popular monthly product review magazine *Consumer Reports* had done a recent write-up. But either possibility could hardly be counted on.

As far as getting the best price, well, for the most part, the price advertised was the price you paid, unless you were willing to wait for a sale or engage in some serious negotiating.

Then this all began to change. Slowly at first. But then faster and faster.

Within a few years, much of what we called *retail* or *shopping* was completely transformed.

THE CANARY IN THE COAL MINE

Having toiled in the retail industry for most of my long career, I'm particularly attuned to its massive upheaval over the past two decades. But it can be a useful, relatable case study for people working in any industry. Retail is one of the biggest parts of any economy, and since we are all regular shoppers, we've had a front-row seat to the rapid evolution of the space.

For better or for worse, how and where we shop also has a profound influence on the culture and the economy. Corporations spend billions to make us crave products regardless of whether we purchase them online or in a brick-and-mortar location. The fashions featured on TV, the movies, the runway, and—increasingly—social media, often define what gets sold online and in the stores we traffic.

Additionally, the sheer size and diversity of retail means it attracts a lot of attention for technology investment. The potential impact from innovations in order processing and tracking, inventory management, payment systems, marketing automation, and the like often have compelling use cases across a spectrum of sectors. So it is not surprising that some of the most obvious and large-scale disruptive forces of digital technology that we now take for granted started to play out in the stores and shopping centers we frequent and on the screens that now command so much of our time and attention.

Slowly but surely, the fundamental bases of competition began to change. As time went on, they became almost unfathomable. Retail success was no longer determined by the best physical location, a well-trained and tenured sales staff, exclusive product distribution rights, or a long-standing reputation in the community. So very many dimensions of what determined success were upended.

ACCESSIBILITY to purveyors of products you might be interested in, once limited by store hours and the number of retailers one was willing to invest the time (and the fuel cost) to visit, shifted to a nearly infinite array of options, available virtually anywhere, at any time, in any way.

PRODUCT CHOICE was no longer limited to what would fit on the shelves of the stores situated in your town—instead, it became a nearly endless aisle of abundance.

INFORMATION about product quality, features and benefits, and in-stock availability (all of which used to be in short supply, cumbersome to acquire and assimilate, and of questionable reliability) was suddenly available in a matter of seconds through search or a direct visit to a staggering number of websites.

PRICE, once largely a take-it-or-leave-it proposition that the vendor decided upon, became less of a given. Prospective buyers' newfound ability to find data on what other customers were paying for a particular item or access to discounts through dedicated websites or browser extensions made finding the best deal much easier. And although discount stores, off-price retail chains, and outlet stores have existed for a long time, totally new, value-oriented concepts emerged both offline and online that contributed to the overall effect of pushing prices down and compressing profit margins.

CONVENIENCE became prized almost as much as a product itself. Before e-commerce growth took off, nearly all retail involved the customer going somewhere to pick up the product. In the cases where products were delivered to a customer's home, either because it was a catalog order or a big-ticket item that typically required home delivery (like a refrigerator, big-screen TV, or sofa), lead times were often long, and upcharges could be significant.

Over time, the number and variety of products that could be delivered to a customer's home or place of business exploded. Simultaneously, the time it took to receive a product continued to shrink. Moreover, inflated delivery fees, once profit centers for many companies, started to disappear completely or were included in frequent free-shipping promotions.

CONNECTION became massively important to the buying experience. Before digital disruption, our connections were largely confined to family, friends, coworkers, and maybe a house of worship or club to which we belonged. Most communication happened face-to-face or over the phone. Today, depending upon how active we are on social media, we may well have many thousands of friends or followers, most of whom we can communicate with instantaneously.

Moreover, new business models have been created based upon this entirely new web of connection. Many of us no longer think about trying out a new restaurant or booking a hotel without first going to sites that crowdsource opinions. So-called sharing economy business models (Uber, Airbnb, etc.) leverage this new phenomenon. The entire resale (or circular economy) market has greatly expanded as companies like thredUP, The RealReal, and Poshmark leverage the power of new connections to marry buyers and sellers of used apparel, accessories, and other items.

This web of connection has also allowed for completely different relationships between companies and their customers. In many cases, it is now possible to have a one-to-one relationship between manufacturer and end consumer. But not only is it possible, it can be highly desirable, as it can radically change the ability to deliver more personal and relevant offerings. It also offers the potential to reshape a company's fundamental economics by leveraging lower-cost digital communications and eliminating the middleman (that is, the cost of employing intermediate distributors of products).

Retail may have been on the leading edge of digital disruption, but looking back, it's hard to see an industry that has not been reshaped by so many of the same forces.

EVERYTHING THAT CAN BE CONNECTED IS CONNECTED

A pre-internet world was a largely disconnected world. If you or your business wanted to be in touch with large numbers of people, collect useful information, access product and service choices, and so on, you'd inevitably butt up against a high degree of friction.

How things have changed. Boundaries that were once

difficult to cross are either gone or readily navigated. Friction (in time, money, or complexity) that we once took for granted is evaporating with every new software update or emerging new business model focused on rooting friction out.

Rishad Tobaccowala, the former chief growth officer at Publicis Groupe and author of *Restoring the Soul of Business*, has posited that in roughly twenty-five years we have already moved into a Third Connected Age.[1] In his telling, from 1993 through 2007 we lived through the First Connected Age, a period characterized by the radically transformed ability to transact via the emergence of e-commerce and the use of search engines to discover previously unavailable or largely inaccessible information. This fundamental shift created many entirely new business models, most notably Amazon and Google.

We entered the Second Connected Age with the advent of smart devices, which meant that vast numbers of people and organizations could be connected 24/7 to vast numbers of other people and organizations virtually (pun intended) anywhere in the world. Here, too, disruptive technology enabled powerful new business models such as the Apple ecosystem, various social media platforms, sharing economy companies, and a new generation of direct-to-consumer, often vertically integrated, brands like Dollar Shave Club, Glossier, and Warby Parker.

The Third Connected Age began to emerge in 2018. 5G allowed for faster connection; virtual and augmented reality and voice commerce created new ways to connect; block-chain, artificial intelligence, and machine learning connected data to data in powerful new ways; and constant, rapid connection via massive computing power unleashed a whole new world of operating in the cloud.

These waves of connection have changed, well, just about everything.

A media landscape of three big television networks and a handful of so-called linear local TV and radio stations has given way to on-demand viewing via Netflix, Hulu, You-Tube, and TikTok. Newspaper advertising, which was the number one category for marketing spending in the late 1990s, has dropped by 52 percent in the last twenty years.[2] Traditional mail shifted to fax to email to text to Snapchat and WhatsApp. Music, games, sports, gambling, and other forms of entertainment are now overwhelmingly consumed digitally.

And on and on.

Across the world, the average person spends some seven hours a day online.[3] Nearly half of US teens now say they use the internet almost constantly.[4] And, quick show of hands: How many of you reading this sleep with your phone nearby and/or are filled with anxiety merely thinking about losing your device?

This pervasive connectedness is probably not awesome for our emotional health, but that doesn't change its truth or how organizations contending with this shift must respond.

The adage that the three most important things in physical real estate are location, location, location no longer resonates in many situations, for either the folks trying to sell something or the customers hoping to buy it.

Today, the best location for brands to engage in is likely wherever our customer happens to be with their trusty device when their thoughts turn to commerce.

Looking back at how all aspects of connection have redefined our everyday lives, it's hard to imagine how much more can change. But it's quite likely that what will unfold over the next decade will make the first three ages of connectedness seem quaint.

For example, until quite recently, few outside of academia and rather obscure R&D departments of technology firms were talking about how potentially game-changing artificial intelligence could be, especially large language models such as ChatGPT. Now, Bill Gates and many others argue that AI's impact could be bigger than the invention of the internet.

WEAPONS OF MASS DISTRACTION

Perhaps you've seen the updated version of Abraham Maslow's hierarchy of needs that puts Wi-Fi access and battery life at the base. It's funny because it's true.

MASLOW'S NEW HIERARCHY OF NEEDS[5]

1	SELF-ACTUALIZATION
2	SELF-ESTEEM
3	LOVE AND BELONGING
4	SAFETY NEEDS
5	PHYSIOLOGICAL NEEDS
6	WI FI
7	BATTERY

To lose access to our devices is to become disconnected from the new world order (figuratively, not in the crazy, conspiracy-minded sense).

Yet gaining access subjects us to a seemingly endless barrage of distractions and stress.

We claim we can multitask, even if the science proves we can't.[6]

If you're anything like me, you have a crazy number of tabs open on your computer and a scary number of unaddressed emails and text messages taunting you.

The fact is, we are living in an *attention economy*, a term coined by psychologist, economist, and Nobel laureate Herbert A. Simon that recognizes that our attention is a scarce resource.[7] We only have so much of it, and there is an epic battle to claim it on the part of friends, family, potential mates, and, most powerfully and often annoyingly, folks trying to sell us something.

Indeed, whether we realize it or not, so much of what we do and how we spend our time is essentially an attempt to get attention.

At our jobs, we might create advertising hoping to bust through the clutter and overcome the veritable tsunami of messaging most people endure constantly.

If we are on online dating apps, we do what we can to avoid the dreaded left swipe.

If we're honest, though, deep down we know we're mostly being ignored. As Steven Pressfield, one of my favorite writers, puts it: "They're not bad people, they're just busy."

But there is a clear, indisputable conclusion we must make if we are trying to become a compelling signal amid all this noise, all this distraction. If we seek to transform, we must accept that attention is finite and we must do something truly remarkable and relevant to break through the clutter, command attention, and earn deep engagement. We must leap to higher ground.

IN COMPETITION WITH THE UNIVERSE

It is not hyperbolic to say we have shifted from a world of relative scarcity in product and service choice to one of staggering, almost incomprehensible, abundance. Our primary competition is no longer the guy across the street or down the road at the mall. In many ways, our world has become both bigger and smaller than we often think.

As previously discussed, for most people in most countries around the world, it can seem like there is an infinite array of customer choice. No longer are we constrained by whatever happens to be carried and in stock in the handful of establishments we are willing to invest our time to drive to. Just about anything we can imagine is available from just about anywhere in the world, and some of it is available to be digitally downloaded in a matter of seconds. The number of products that can be delivered to our home or office the next day (or in some cases, within an hour or two) has gone up by multiple orders of magnitude in the past three decades.

As e-commerce became a growing force, some products, like music, books, and games, could be delivered digitally and had, for all intents and purposes, no incremental inventory carrying, warehousing, and transportation costs. This allowed retailers like Amazon to offer a virtually endless aisle, constrained more by computing power than by literal shelf space.

Mail-order catalogs, both consumer-facing (think L.L. Bean, Lands' End, etc.) and business-to-business (Grainger, Ferguson, etc.), pioneered a strategy of offering greater product choice than their brick-and-mortar-centric brethren. Their model of marketing via direct mail and largely avoiding physical store distribution allowed them to cost-effectively stock products in large regional warehouses rather than expensive real estate on the high street or in high-rent shopping centers.

The huge growth in third-party marketplaces has only expanded this ecosystem further. Demand is aggregated on a primary brand's site, be it business-to-consumer or business-to-business, but fulfillment is generally provided by another company. Over 60 percent of Amazon's retail sales now come from third-party vendors,[8] and many other companies are adopting this model to greatly expand their assortments without having to invest in inventory and other expensive support costs.

The shift from needing to be slightly better than our fiercest local competitor to win the sale to having to be best-in-class compared with a vast array of competitors who might be almost anywhere in the world has been, in a word, profound.

A CONFEDERACY OF MEH

The result is a world where there is often too much of everything and not nearly enough of anything truly remarkable.

When I talk about *remarkable*, I mean it in the way that Seth Godin advanced in his groundbreaking 2003 book *Purple Cow*. There is the common meaning of the word: something remarkable is highly unique, quite different, unusual. But the secret sauce, the top spin, the X factor, is the other sense of the word: something remarkable literally causes people to remark upon it.

If we are going to find our way out of the boring, undifferentiated middle, we're going to have to do more than simply satisfy our customers' needs at a decent price. Existing loyalties are often quite set. Our ideal prospects typically have plenty of decent alternatives to what we sell. We must take our game to a whole new level.

If you want a glaring example of what remarkable doesn't look like, walk through a typical large mall. During your stroll, you won't have a hard time picking out dozens of shops that seem designed for an era that no longer exists. Visit one of the midpriced anchor stores and you might feel like you've accidentally wandered into The Museum of Disappointment.

For a long time, serving the peak of the bell curve, chasing the largest possible audience, and making average stuff for average people was a winning strategy. When it was harder to access ready substitutes, the sheer volume of options was far lower; and customers couldn't surf the internet to get useful, reliable information about our product or service, we could get away with being merely very good, or just marginally better than average. Frankly, sometimes even just barely serviceable. Customers would settle because for all practical purposes they had to. They literally had no choice.

Today, the situation is clearly very different. Today, if we aren't truly remarkable, not only do we not get the sale but we may not even get noticed in the first place. And even if we command a prospective customer's attention, if all we offer is rather average, there is almost certainly someone willing to offer the same thing at a lower price. Trying to be everything can often end up not being very much of anything.

THE COLLAPSE OF THE UNREMARKABLE MIDDLE

Too many companies remain married to the mob, pursuing a largely one-size-fits-all strategy that typically results in one-size-underwhelms-many.

The first time I started to wonder if focusing on the vast middle of the market was a sustainable strategy was when I was still at Sears. Even some twenty years ago it looked more and more like success was being found at either end of a spectrum.

At one end were companies that largely focused on lower prices, convenience, a wide assortment of choices, and ease of transacting. At the other end were brands that leaned into a unique product or service offering, high levels of customer service, and generally more of an upscale or premium experience.

Somewhere in the huge, messy, increasingly muddy middle sat Sears. And they were hardly alone in being a company that had historically served the peak of the bell curve and was finding it harder and harder to deliver strong results.

Back in 2011, after I had left Neiman Marcus and gone out on my own as a consultant, I wrote a piece for my newly created blog titled "Death in the Middle." In it, I observed that retailers that catered neither to the affluent customer nor to the price- and value-oriented one seemed to be experiencing ever-worsening fortunes.

As I ventured out into the keynote speaking world, I began talking about this as "retail's great bifurcation." It became ever more apparent that success was being found at either end of the value spectrum, but trying to win in the vast and messy middle ground was becoming darn near untenable, leading me to explore this topic further in a piece for *Forbes*.[9]

Then, in 2018, my friends at Deloitte put a lot more meat on the bones of my theory with their in-depth study with a similar title.[10] Their data clearly showed that "price-based" retailers in the United States were adding lots of new locations and growing their sales nicely. Similarly, "premium" retailers were also opening many locations and experiencing strong revenue growth. Yet those that Deloitte (quite generously) labeled "balanced" (i.e., those that offered neither a strong value-oriented proposition nor anything special from a product, service, or experience perspective) were shrinking both their store fleets as well as their relative market share.

This general pattern of strength at either end of the spectrum continues to play out. As we've seen during the past few years, bankruptcies, liquidations, and mass store closings (Toys"R"Us, JCPenney, Sears, Bed Bath & Beyond, Rite Aid, and more) continue to be overwhelming concentrated in the unremarkable middle.

This bifurcation is hardly limited to retail. The hotel business has seen an explosion of new concepts. Marriott and Hyatt have all launched various sub-brands over the years, aiming both high and low, while their more generic nameplates are de-emphasized. In the airline industry, consolidation continues among the big carriers, and newer entrants are focused on either the more value- and convenience-oriented segment (Breeze, Avelo, PLAY) or the higher-end one (JSX, Aero).

POWER FLIPS

Most of the history of capitalism and business strategy as practiced for centuries saw power and control largely and firmly in the hands of brand owners. Companies marketed and sold to customers. They designed and sourced the product, assembled a distribution network, created brand and promotional campaigns, put together a media plan (even if they didn't call it that), and so on. What customers ultimately perceived and felt about a brand was heavily influenced by what companies invested gobs of money into persuading them to think. It was overwhelmingly a one-way street, a process predicated far more on push than pull.

Seth Godin does a great job boiling this down:

> The non-networked world was driven by push.
> The merchant stocked goods and waited for you to come buy them. The manufacturer made things in advance and advertised so you'd go buy them. The cab waited by the corner hoping you'd come out and hail it.
> The door-to-door salesperson went door to door.
> But the web amplifies pull instead. When you need something, you tell Google or Amazon or Lyft or Shopify and they bring it to you. The ratio of inventory to demand has shifted dramatically—instead of one encyclopedia in every single house that sits idly waiting for you to need it, there's just one Wikipedia, available to be pulled by anyone, at will.[11]
>
> —SETH GODIN

This fundamental shift can be best seen as more of a flip, putting much more power in the hands of individuals (and the groups they are or seek to be affiliated with) while weakening the hegemony of brands and organizations.

A company may tell us their hotel is amazing, but let's go see what TripAdvisor has to say. An airline may try to gaslight the public on a customer service issue, but let's see how this plays out on social media. If we want to see a vast array of options, let's not go to a brand web page, but instead do a filtered search on an aggregation site to compare and contrast our choices.

A brand is no longer what we tell the consumer it is—it is what consumers tell each other it is.

—SCOTT COOK, COFOUNDER OF INTUIT

Customers are no longer constrained by one-way, often asymmetric sources of information. And with increased knowledge, they have dramatically amplified power. For businesses, this can be terrifying—or an opportunity.

The right response to fear of change isn't doubling down or pretending nothing's happening. By this point, I think you know where both lead. The proper response is to open our minds and try something new, something bold. The seven mind leaps that I discuss in Part Two will prepare you to do just that.

RESISTANCE IS FUTILE

You may not like the present state of affairs, or you may not fully appreciate how revolutionary these shifts truly are. But fighting them is like fighting gravity. It's a battle you cannot win.

You can cut all the flowers, but you cannot keep spring from coming.

—PABLO NERUDA

The challenge is not to figure out how to mount resistance, but to accept the things you cannot change, get focused on the things you can, and then get to work.

It's become fashionable, particularly as the world reeled from the impact of a global pandemic, to say we have entered a "new normal." I've always hated this. There is no "normal" or "new normal" or even "next normal." There is only *now*.

And right now, if we're honest, things are quite volatile, uncertain, and more than a bit scary. But if you can meet the challenge of our current age—and it is a mighty one—your expiration date need not come due.

Shift happens. Get used to it.

Shift happens. Shake hands with the new weird.

Shift happens. Don't let it destroy your future.

Shift happens. Summon up all the courage you require.

Shift happens. Choose remarkable.

Shift happens. Get ready to leap.

CHAPTER 2

THE CURSE OF THE TIMID TRANSFORMATION

If you do not change direction,
you may end up where you are heading.

—LAO TZU

Q: HOW MANY PSYCHOLOGISTS DOES IT TAKE TO CHANGE A LIGHT BULB? A: One, but the light bulb has to want to change. And so it goes with organizations and the executives who lead them, if they are serious about transformation.

Of course, pretty much everybody says they want to change. In fact, every organization I have ever worked with on their innovation and growth strategy, and virtually every senior leader I have ever advised, doesn't just say they want to change—they insist they have no choice. They *must* change (sometimes pounding their desk for special emphasis).

Survey after survey backs me up. As just one example, according to the AlixPartners study I referenced in the introduction, 98 percent of CEOs agree that investing in new technology and digital solutions must be a priority. That's a lot of CEOs. We're talking North Korea election numbers.

Yet, as one of my more insightful colleagues puts it (and I'm paraphrasing): We all say we want to change. But what we really want is to keep doing what we always have done, just a bit better.

Indeed, far too many leaders put forward a transformation agenda that is merely applying totally unnecessary cosmetics to a rather stocky domesticated animal. And even if the changes they support are fundamentally sound, they often put them into place far too slowly.

As an experienced bullshit-dispelling enthusiast, I often find myself triggered by the words of many a decidedly mediocre company CEO sharing their latest inventor presentation or earnings update. They will present their multi-point, long-term growth strategy as if they have created some magical elixir to unlock a phenomenally better future.

Instead, what they advance as a bold change agenda is mostly designed to address things they should have tackled years earlier or seeks to close gaps in areas where the competition has already built a sizable advantage.

Though I try to keep my schadenfreude in check, inevitably the voice of an airline captain from a recent flight begins taking over my mind: "Ladies and gentlemen, we're about to begin our initial descent."

It's never too early to panic.

—LEN GOODMAN

BAILING DOESN'T FIX THE HOLE

Let's look at the troubled department store sector. Consider that the three biggest American national chains (Macy's, Kohl's, and JCPenney) have all breathlessly espoused various new turnaround strategies for years. CEOs have come and gone—as I write this, JCPenney is on its fourth in under ten years—and yet despite new executives, tons of investment, revamped programs, and so on, it's all added up to nothing of any real significance.

But it's actually worse than that. Not only have the various attempts at transformation failed to gain any real traction, but their lackluster efforts (particularly in the case of Macy's and JCPenney) have forced them to close hundreds of stores and engage in significant cost cutting. Although addressing structural cost issues can often be necessary, one thing we know for sure is that closing stores makes shopping a lot less convenient for those customers affected. "But can't they just shop online?" you might ask. As it turns out, closing stores most often reduces overall e-commerce sales in the trade area where a location has been shuttered. This is because stores serve as valuable advertising for a brand or as a showroom for products, regardless of where the customer decides to transact. Increasingly popular features like "Buy online, pick up in store" or "Buy online, return to store" no longer become factors in customers choosing a particular brand over the competition when a nearby store is no longer an option.

It also turns out that massive cuts in operating budgets can make a bad situation even worse. If you've ever tried to find someone to help you at some of these stores, witnessed the ragged appearance of their shop floors, or noticed the large number of products out of stock, you know precisely what I mean.

When I am delivering a keynote, I will often ask the audience whether they can name one company that has successfully cost-cut and store-closed their way to prosperity.

Bueller? Bueller? Bueller?

More times than most leaders will own up to, what they refer to as a "growth strategy" or "transformation agenda" doesn't do much of anything to address the hole that is causing them to leak market share to the competition. Bailing doesn't fix the hole. And when we think it does, we merely become the architects of our own misfortune.

Half measures availed us nothing.
—THE BIG BOOK OF ALCOHOLICS ANONYMOUS

WHAT TOOK YOU SO LONG?

During the depths of the COVID pandemic, we witnessed a tremendous (and unusual) amount of innovation on the part of many organizations. Companies across many industries embraced new ways to communicate, fulfill orders, take payments, and a whole lot more. I personally know of several organizations that had been slow-walking various pilot programs and were suddenly hit with a bolt of urgency to roll them out. Desperation can do that sometimes.

But if seismic shifts have been rippling through your

organization for well over a decade—if you've had a hard time winning, growing, and keeping customers for years, and your default response to difficulties with growing the top line has been to reflexively engage in another round of cost cutting—why did you wait for a gut punch to take bold, decisive action?

It shouldn't take a crisis to innovate.

Aside from innovations that addressed coronavirus-specific issues, any idea that worked well during the pandemic probably would have been a good idea to roll out much earlier. As just one small example, many companies experienced enormous success by offering "Buy online, pick up in store," known in the industry as BOPIS. At both retailers where I led strategy, we initially made this feature available more than fifteen years ago.

If the pandemic caused you to finally offer this service, then good on you, but don't pretend that what you did is innovative. The real question is what took you so long.

INNOVATING TO PARITY

One reason meaningful transformation can be so hard is that up to a certain point, change isn't transformation—it's merely keeping up. What used to distinguish a brand's performance a few years ago is now often a requirement or has already become completely uninteresting or largely irrelevant.

When I first began working in e-commerce in the late 1990s, standard product delivery times were about a week. If you wanted expedited delivery, we charged a hefty fee and often made a nice profit. Over time, free delivery (and often product returns) became a basic customer expectation. Moreover, today many products can be delivered the same day or sometimes in less than an hour.

Being able to see a nearby store's inventory, use your smartphone to check into a hotel, find detailed product information in a matter of seconds, or get text reminders about your upcoming doctor's appointment were once novel features. Now they are increasingly expected.

And on and on.

Customers' expectations continue to be ratcheted up. The bar for essential competitive performance continues to be raised. What was once a source of differentiation has become a starting point. But don't confuse the absolute necessity to execute well against basic customer requirements with actual innovation. Merely closing competitive gaps is not sufficient to keep pace with the speed of disruption.

As the pace of change accelerates, our list of necessary actions is likely to be rather long. They may take quite a lot of time and consume substantial resources to bring to life. But we must be careful not to confuse table stakes with differentiators.

When our best is merely average, we risk falling farther and farther behind.

WHO WANTS A FASTER HORSE?

Henry Ford turned out to be a terribly flawed human being in many ways. Yet, in addition to being the father of the mass-produced automobile in the United States, he is responsible for a quotation that is insightful and has survived the test of time: "If I had asked people what they wanted, they would have said faster horses."

When it comes to real transformation, the organizations that fail to make sufficient progress, that remain hopelessly stuck in the past, so often fall into the faster-horse trap.

Truly disruptive business models—the ones that create remarkable and highly valuable brands—rarely focus on doing the same thing that has always been done but just somewhat faster or a bit cheaper. Instead, they solve customer issues in profound new ways.

Uber isn't simply a new and improved taxi service; they get customers from point A to point B in a fundamentally different way. Airbnb isn't another hotel chain; it rewires the entire supply system of how people experience a location when traveling. The list goes on.

The faster-horse approach is optimizing a current way of delivering value. It is doing exactly the same thing, just a bit better. But if your current model is at or approaching its expiration date, a slightly better version of it will not only fail to make a difference over the longer term: it will also distract you from taking the necessary leaps you must.

Being the best blacksmith in town was a pretty great gig. Until it wasn't.

SLOW, AFRAID, AND CLINGING TO THE PAST

Have you ever seen a timid trapeze artist?

Of course not. There aren't any; they either get fired or they get killed.

If you hesitate when leaping from one rope to another, you're not going to last very long.

And this is at the heart of what makes innovation work in organizations, why industries die, and how painful it is to try to maintain the status quo while also participating in a revolution.

Gather up as much speed as you can, find a path and let go. You can't get to the next rope if you're still holding on to this one.[1]

—SETH GODIN

I've worked with and observed quite a few leaders who have spent their careers sitting on the fence. They talked a lot about the need to innovate, to transform for an emerging era, and yet it remained overwhelmingly a whole lot of talk and very little progress.

My intention isn't to bash them here. Truly. I recognize and respect the pressures they faced, from investors to boards to colleagues to employees to customers. It's easy to come down hard on these leaders. But it's also easy to see why so many of us fail to act even if we can see the need for change and extol its virtues.

We often work in ossified organizational cultures that push back against substantive efforts to evolve.

Established compensation structures may tend to reward short-term performance over long-term investment.

The demands of Wall Street may reinforce an obsessive

focus on hitting quarterly targets.

And, as we'll delve into later, fear of failure, imposter syndrome, and all manner of societal pressures conspire to keep us stuck.

As the pace of change accelerates, as the gap widens between what customers demand and what you are prepared to offer, those who hesitate are indeed lost.

Sunk costs are sunk.

Opportunity costs are real.

It's scary to let go of what made us successful in the past to leap into an uncertain future.

It is demonstrably hard to know exactly what to do when things are changing so quickly.

But you know what else is hard? Having to close stores and lay off thousands of employees because we were too timid in our willingness to do the things that might have preserved those locations and saved those jobs. Trust me, I've been there, and it was probably the lowest point in a career that's had many difficult moments.

If the market is kicking your ass and you're finding it hard to acquire new customers or to get current customers to advocate strongly for your brand, then it's worth asking yourself: why am I working so hard to defend the status quo?

The greatest danger in times of turbulence is not the turbulence; it's acting with yesterday's logic.

—PETER DRUCKER

WELCOME TO THE GRAND DELUSION

As the (not terribly good) joke goes, denial ain't a river in Egypt.

Yet failure to accept reality is an incredibly persistent, powerful, and pernicious force in many people's lives, including yours truly. I'll leave the therapy to those professionally trained to diagnose and treat it, but those who sign up for transformations that stand little or no chance of working are often completely disconnected from the truth of their situations.

'Tis but a flesh wound.

—THE BLACK KNIGHT TO ARTHUR
IN *MONTY PYTHON AND THE HOLY GRAIL*

Sometimes a timid transformation arises from our failure to grasp just how much we must reimagine our business model if we're going to win the future. So, we must ask ourselves: Is the degree to which we are changing profound enough to grow and keep the customers we need to achieve our long-term success?

Sometimes a timid transformation arises from the belief that a slow and steady pace of innovation can close any competitive gaps that need to be addressed. So, we must ask ourselves: Even if our transformation agenda has the potential to exceed customer expectations, are we doing it nearly fast enough?

Sometimes a timid transformation arises from the belief

that what brought us success in the past will serve us well in executing what we need to do going forward. So, we must ask ourselves: Have we let go of what we must to future-proof our organization?

If the recent past is a useful teacher (spoiler alert: it most certainly is), we can see that many of the companies that are failing to transform at the speed of disruption have simply not been telling themselves the truth.

I long for the day when a CEO starts out an investor presentation with something like this: "In recent years, we have not experienced the same level of growth that we saw in the past, not because we have changed, but because we have not changed enough."

THE OPPOSITE IS RISKY

Not that it's probably news to you, but humans tend to be rather averse to risk. It turns out that evolutionary biology has hardwired caution into our nervous systems. Much of this is driven by the amygdala, the part of our brain also known as the "lizard brain." This prehistoric part of the brain helps drive some of our base emotions, including fear. It's responsible for what you likely know as the "flight, fight, or freeze" response. This reflexive reaction is super helpful when a bear is charging toward you, but not so much when it comes to tackling more common fears.

Combine this with the fact that most human beings assess short-term trade-offs pretty well but typically struggle to act on longer-term, sustained efforts, even when the facts and logic are compelling and indisputable. For example, most people know that their risk of early death is much greater if they have a poor diet and don't exercise. But in the moment, digging into those French fries while binge-watching the latest Netflix series may well win out.

In the same way, companies that embark on a too-timid transformation agenda fundamentally misunderstand risk. They believe that incremental improvements and a slow and steady, more evolutionary approach to strategic change is the best way to mitigate risk. But as we see time and time again from companies that have been pounding away at turnaround efforts for years with little to show for it, this approach is not a saving grace. Half measures are not enough.

When a large gap emerges between our plans and what customers desire and the competition delivers, it is time to leap. We must boldly and decisively move up and to the right. Failure to do so is choosing the riskiest path of all.

The biggest risk is not taking any risk. . . . In a world that is changing really quickly, the only strategy that is guaranteed to fail is not taking any risks.

—MARK ZUCKERBERG

Even worse is doubling down on a losing hand. An escalating commitment to a failing course of action is an all-too-common response from companies that find themselves under siege from insurgent competition. Blockbuster's reaction to the emergence of Netflix is a great example. All this does is make it that much harder to pull out of the inevitable dive.

PREPARE FOR LIFTOFF

Does every organization need to adopt a strategy of radical change?

Probably not. There are areas of the economy that have been largely insulated from the forces of disruption and the seismic shifts we have discussed thus far. (For the time being, at least. Talk to me in five years.)

Must every leader have an epiphany to have any chance of guiding their organizations to and over the next mountain?

That's unlikely, too.

The degree and pace of your transformation might be exactly where it needs to be.

Or it may not.

In some cases, it may not take a massive reimagination to get ambitious transformation plans that have stalled or been derailed back on track.

In most situations, however, the way forward requires us to adopt a true paradigm shift. We need a reboot on how we approach disruptive innovation. We need to hit reset on our transformation efforts.

Ctrl. Alt. Delete.[2]

As mentioned at the outset, our goals for our organization need to be reframed. We must aim higher, move faster, and act more boldly.

We need to leap.

Up and to the right.

It's one thing to sign up for a BHAG ("big, hairy, audacious goal"). It's another to take action that propels you forward.

This is where Part Two comes in.

It's where I describe and advocate for seven mind leaps leaders must make to create a more remarkable future. They

CHAPTER 2

are important enough that I've devoted a full chapter to each.

Mind Leap 1: **Crush Your Ego**
Mind Leap 2: **Wake Up**
Mind Leap 3: **Special, Not Big**
Mind Leap 4: **Start with Wow**
Mind Leap 5: **Think Radically**
Mind Leap 6: **Safe Is Risky**
Mind Leap 7: **Faster, Faster, Go, Go, Go!**

They all demand that we let go of the way many of us have typically operated and led. Collectively, they provide the catalysts—one might even say the jet fuel—that can enable us to transform at the speed of disruption.

If we are to win the battle between being remarkable or being irrelevant, if we are to avoid the curse of the timid transformation—if we are to truly lead—our only choice is to leap.

PART 2

THE SEVEN
LEADERSHIP
MIND LEAPS

CHAPTER 3

MIND LEAP 1:
CRUSH YOUR EGO

GET HUMBLE. EMBRACE VULNERABILITY.
BE WILLING TO ASK FOR HELP.

There is an enemy. That enemy is you.

—STEVEN PRESSFIELD

IF YOU ARE ANYTHING LIKE ME, you've been conditioned to believe that through sheer focus, the right education, hard work, and fierce determination, you can accomplish just about anything—that you can be a nearly omnipotent master of your own domain.

Be productive. Stay focused. Never let them see you sweat. Don't let too much space exist between you and your job.

Plan the work. Work the plan. Rinse and repeat.

I'm going to argue that there's a better way to develop yourself and to lead others.

It demands making a conceptual shift from self-centered notions of power and control to something quite different.

I don't do this to be provocative. I do this because I firmly believe that failure to make this shift creates a profound barrier to nearly any sustained efforts to change—in our personal lives, in our roles as leaders, or in any worthy and challenging endeavor.

So far I've kept things comparatively abstract. Now it's time to get specific and, dare I say, more intimate.

I'm going to argue that while it is understandable to believe that successful transformations are often hindered by poor analysis, cultural barriers, not enough innovative ideas, a lack of appropriate resources, poor board support, extreme pressure to meet quarterly earnings, and maybe even the occasional black-swan event, it is very often the case that progress is impeded by that person we see in the mirror each day.

In other words, our relentless attachment to ego can make true transformation impossible. To move forward, to leap to a new plateau, we must be willing to let go.

I'M THE PROBLEM. IT'S ME.

About fifteen years ago, I had what I'll charitably call a crisis of confidence. After spending years successfully climbing the corporate ladder, I hit a wall. Hard.

I had been on a pretty awesome professional trajectory for more than two decades, which, in my midthirties, included being named the youngest vice president and division general manager ever at an iconic, century-old retailer, and then, just a few years later, being elected an executive officer at one of the most prestigious retailers in the world.

Despite this, my career, and just about everything else around me, all came crashing down.

Not only had I resigned from a position that, at that time, seemed perfect for me, but because I allowed my career success to become so intertwined with how I viewed my general worthiness as a human being, losing my job meant I had also lost myself.

I sank into a very deep and dark hole of depression. Looking back on things now, I would say I experienced something between a complete spiritual collapse and an abject mental breakdown.

Ultimately, the gory details aren't all that important (besides, I need to leave some gas in the tank for my rip-roaring, tell-all memoir). But I will share that it was incredibly painful for me, my family, and pretty much everyone around me, and it had all been building for quite a long time. Similar to many people's situations, how and why it all went down the particular way it did was, shall we say, complicated.

Regardless, it took a lot of time, focus, and effort to right the ship and to discover—with the help of many amazing friends, therapists, and spiritual teachers—the root of my problems.

It wasn't simply a highly dysfunctional and chaotic childhood, a lack of appreciation on the part of my bosses, a paucity of support from what I saw as jealous or overly competitive colleagues, terribly bad luck, or any of the dozens of excuses I'd made over the years to keep feeling like a victim and to prevent me from taking a hard look in the mirror.

My ego was the enemy. And until I accepted that completely, very little of any consequence was going to change.

Many of us insist the main impediment to a full, successful life is the outside world. In fact, the most common enemy lies within our ego. Early in our careers it impedes learning and the cultivation of talent. With success it can blind us to our faults and sow future problems. In failure, it magnifies each blow and makes recovery more difficult. At every stage, ego holds us back.

—RYAN HOLIDAY, *EGO IS THE ENEMY*

To be sure, my family history of mental illness played a not-insignificant part. But even there my ego got in the way, as I spent literally decades being too proud or too ashamed to ask for help.

I've had the good fortune of working with many top-performing, hard-charging executives. I've also studied and written about many more type A leaders during the past fifteen years. Were there times when they failed or behaved poorly because of bad judgment, ignorance, or sheer stupidity?

Absolutely.

At the same time, many leaders suffer from what I call executive ego dysfunction. It's a close cousin of narcissistic personality disorder but doesn't require a clinical diagnosis. We pretty much know when we see or experience it in a leader: an exaggerated sense of their knowledge and insight, a need to always be the center of attention, an unwillingness to ask for help, and so on. I bet you can rather easily think of a few high-profile leaders who fit this description.

All too often we ignore their dysfunction because of their presumed genius, outsized financial results, huge social media following, or overall celebrity. For the sake of humanity and our own serenity, we shouldn't.

I ALONE CAN FIX IT

Like me, you were probably taught at an early age that self-sufficiency was a virtue. If you went, as I did, to a famous school and upon graduation joined a prestigious company, you got the sense that you were, hmmm, how should I phrase it? Pretty hot shit.

Although teamwork was formally deemed important in most of the roles I had early in my career, I quickly learned that doing things that called attention to my obvious awesomeness was by far the main way one got ahead. Once I joined a large corporation, the hierarchy was clear, as were the means to get noticed, get bonuses, get promoted, and end up in the corner office. As one mentor put it to me before I had even turned thirty: "It's a dog-eat-dog world, son, and only one person gets the big job."

As I started to get those bigger and bigger jobs, the notion that I was the supreme source of power and wisdom—the main man, the head honcho, the grand pooh-bah—was constantly reinforced. My subordinates often hung on to my every word (or so it seemed) or worked hard to figure out just what it was that "the boss" wanted. I'm also quite certain I was guilty of more mansplaining than anyone should be subjected to.

As time went on, I found myself with a seat at the table in

more and more of the rooms where it happened: Strategic planning discussions and large allocations of capital. Annual budget reviews. Presentations to the board of directors of publicly traded companies worth many billions of dollars. Important people seemed to listen to what I had to say. They trusted me with huge sums of money and the oversight of many hundreds of people. And the money as well as the impressive-sounding titles just kept coming.

I don't have a diagnosis of narcissistic personality disorder, but let's just say any narcissistic tendencies I have were very much reinforced by the system I was part of. That's hardly a coincidence. The traditional leadership model for many legacy organizations thrives on creating an "up or out" dynamic. Cultural norms, built over generations, reinforce the nearly mythical qualities ascribed to those who ascend to the thrones of well-known organizations.

I also seemed to have an almost pathological draw to difficult situations and nearly impossible challenges.

Have a business that needs to be turned around? Hey, I'll do it!

Need to jump-start a moribund division that's lost its way? Ooh, pick me, pick me!

Want to energize the growth potential of an ill-advised acquisition? Baby, I'm your man.

After a while you begin to believe your own press. I know I did.

Of course, it's not just me.

We've made godlike figures out of CEOs, founding entrepreneurs, and other leaders we treat like rock stars, and all too often the results are not pretty. We've all seen countless examples of leaders who fall prey to the Dunning–Kruger effect: the tendency of people to overestimate their competence in areas outside of their core expertise.

Whatever the reason, it's a really bad idea to get high on your own supply. I learned this the hard way, but you don't have to.

The truth you believe and cling to makes you unavailable to hear anything new.

—PEMA CHÖDRÖN

WE'RE FATED TO PRETEND

Executive ego dysfunction often has a seemingly contrary symptom. Although we may feel all-powerful, like complete masters of our domain who are always fully in charge, deep down many of us suffer from bouts of imposter syndrome. It's really two sides of the same coin.

Imposter syndrome is often defined as the frequent or persistent feeling that our success is not deserved. Even worse, we may be deathly afraid that at any time somebody is going to discover we have little or no idea what we are doing.

When we are feeling the shame of not being good enough, a lot of coping styles can start driving the bus, as Dr. Valerie Young has researched.[1] We can become a *perfectionist*, working hard to not make even a single mistake that could expose us as a fraud. We can become the *rugged individualist*, taking on everything ourselves so no one ever has a chance to spot a weakness. Another style is the *expert*. Here, we go overboard on research and analysis so that our argument is bulletproof. Or we may go into *superhero* mode, working ourselves to the bone so we don't miss anything.

These forms of coping manifest differently than being overly confident in our abilities, but they are just as powerful in getting in the way of effective leadership and can be particularly detrimental when it comes to driving transformation efforts. Our insecurities can keep us horribly stuck—if we let them.

YOU'RE PROBABLY WRONG

As leaders, much of our compensation (both monetary and psychological) comes from being right. But there's a problem with being right.

When we are convinced we are right, we often grasp too tightly to getting our way, becoming overly attached to the outcome. I used to joke that I was always one new iteration of a PowerPoint deck away from persuading anybody of anything. It's a bit of an exaggeration, but honestly not by much.

There is also a good chance that you are, in fact, wrong. Not necessarily wildly and irresponsibly wrong, but when we assume we have all the answers, we close ourselves off to other points of view or other more valuable possibilities.

We learn nothing by being right.
—ELIZABETH BIBESCO

Having been the head of strategy at two Fortune 500 companies, and now a strategy advisor, author, and keynote speaker, making recommendations and trying to persuade folks to adopt what I advance as deep insight and wisdom is pretty much my job. For most of my life, I acted as if I were supremely confident that I was right and believed that if I could not convince you, I was a failure.

Being much less certain that we have all the answers may not be celebrated in most corporate cultures, but it is necessary to get better results from your innovation efforts. It also has the side benefit of decreasing the odds that you will drive yourself and those around you insane.

The world is divided into people who think they are right.

—DENNIS SPARKS

THE WISDOM OF UNCERTAINTY

As leaders, many of us are taught to be confident, to exude certainty, to never let them see us sweat. Any wavering is seen as weakness.

But absolute certainty does not exist. And lack of it is neither good nor bad. Uncertainty is neutral.

In an uncertain world, it is not surprising that we seek the safety of knowing something for sure. But mostly it is a trap our ego beckons us into.

Embracing uncertainty creates a sense of wonder, of discernment, of curiosity—all incredibly valuable skills for driving creativity and seeing a wider range of options and actions. Pushing back and challenging those places where we feel certain helps us unlock limiting beliefs that may keep us stuck.

Consider all the beliefs that the auto industry held on to that kept them from embracing electric vehicles far earlier. Or those in the taxi industry who mostly sat around and watched Uber and Lyft transform their industry. Or the folks at BlackBerry who hung on to the idea that a mobile phone must have a keyboard while the iPhone revolutionized the ways we communicate.

What we often need to do is not learn or study more in an attempt to become more certain, but to unlearn what we believe to be unchangeable so that infinite potential has a chance to reveal itself.

Most importantly, we must cultivate what Zen Buddhists call *shoshin*, or "beginner's mind." Beginner's mind means letting go of certainty and taking on an attitude of openness, eagerness, and lack of bias when studying, much as a beginner would.

Experienced leaders, like all mortals, struggle with preconceived notions, confirmation bias, blind spots, and a belief that what has made them successful in the past is likely to serve them well in the future. Many of us carry around a very particular hammer, hoping to pound a very particular set of nails. But we need to be careful what we worship—be it money, power, fame, or any other thing or belief that impedes our progress. For that which we worship, we risk becoming.

In the beginner's mind there are many possibilities, but in the expert's there are few.

—SHUNRYU SUZUKI

In his brilliant book *Think Again: The Power of Knowing What You Don't Know*, bestselling author and Wharton professor Adam Grant stresses the importance of intellectual humility, curiosity, and a willingness to challenge our own beliefs to become more successful in navigating the future.

In one chapter he points to three things we cling to at the expense of being open to possibilities that may serve us better. They're worth summarizing here:

ASSUMPTIONS: Grant emphasizes the need to question our assumptions and be open to changing our beliefs when new evidence or perspectives emerge. He argues that many of our assumptions are based on outdated information or biases, and by challenging them, we can discover new insights and make better decisions.

INSTINCTS: He encourages readers to be cautious of relying solely on their gut feelings. Although instincts can be valuable in certain situations, they can also lead us astray, particularly when faced with complex or unfamiliar problems.

HABITS: Grant suggests that our habits can sometimes hinder our ability to think critically and adapt to new information. He advocates for a mindset of continuous learning and growth, which involves being open to feedback, actively seeking out new perspectives, and being willing to unlearn and relearn.

When I read this section of the book, I was caught between two strong emotions: satisfaction that he had articulated something so important and bitterness that I hadn't realized it earlier in my career, when my ego was in full protection mode.

WINNING THE OVARIAN LOTTERY

Humility isn't a good policy just because we don't know what we don't know. Or because we're all subject to a tangle of biases, wrong assumptions, and bad habits. It's also because we may be far luckier than we realize—or care to admit.

Billionaire Warren Buffett reminds us to not discount the role blind luck plays in our good fortunes, specifically the time, place, and conditions under which we were born. It's an idea derived from philosopher John Rawls's classic *A Theory of Justice* and likely influenced by the concept of "ovarian roulette" from psychologist Dr. Reginald Lourie.[2]

Related to this notion is the saying "Some people are born on third base and go through life thinking they hit a triple," which is generally attributed to football coach Barry Switzer.

It's possible that you weren't born into a position of considerable privilege and that literally everything good that's ever happened to you is completely a function of your hard work, resilience, genius, and devastatingly charming personality. It's possible, but it's not likely.

This is not to say you haven't earned much of what you accomplished. But our ego is great at propping up the "I deserve it" story and conveniently ignoring the role of serendipity and advantages that were granted to us for whatever reason.

Is it just possible that someone else did all the right things, just like you, but things turned out very differently for them? (That's a rhetorical question.)

GRAY IS MY NEW FAVORITE COLOR

Few things are as black and white as they seem. But as leaders we are often trained to see them as such. Working or not. Right or wrong. Profitable or unprofitable. Do you want to go with this, or do you want to go with that?

Related to the idea of the wisdom of uncertainty is letting go of dualistic thinking and accepting that there is a lot more texture and nuance to much of what we need to deal with. Transformation is messy, and the right answer, the preferred course of action, is rarely all that clear from the outset.

We need to wade in murky waters and walk down many misty avenues before clarity of action will reveal itself. In later chapters I will suggest how mind leaps can help us accelerate our journey. But as we get started down a new path, finding greater humility and letting go of rigid views of how the world works will set us up to leap successfully.

CAN I BE REAL A SECOND?
FOR JUST A MILLISECOND?

Until quite recently, *vulnerability* was not a word that got used very much when it came to desirable leadership qualities. Although I have not done an exhaustive search, I doubt that it appears much in the work of highly regarded corporate strategists, innovation specialists, or those who claim to be futurists.

There are many definitions of vulnerability. For me, it has come to mean having the emotional courage to expose myself and be seen for who I really am and what is really going on with me.

In every place I have ever worked, being vulnerable was not discussed—it was tacitly (and often overtly) discouraged. I was taught from an early age not to show my emotions and mostly to figure out things for myself. In my corporate experience, the messages were *work hard*, *suck it up*, and *keep your personal stuff to yourself*.

But it's clearly not just where I have happened to work. We are surrounded by messages that to be vulnerable is to be weak. Hustle porn is a regular feature of popular personal productivity books, YouTube videos, and social media posts. Clearly it's more than a gendered issue, but the notion of vulnerability as a desirable trait, particularly for those who identify as men, is undercut by toxic, old-fashioned ideas of what it means to be a man.

Aside from the vast psychological damage this can do— and here I very much speak from personal experience— failure to be vulnerable closes us off from so many possibilities. If we are willing to bravely bring people into any creative process or complex problem-solving endeavor, we are almost certain to leap to places far beyond where we could go on our own.

I cannot possibly do justice to this topic in a few hundred words. For a far deeper dive, I would point you to Brené Brown's amazing work on this subject and more broadly on the topic of courageous leadership. But I wholeheartedly believe that to create the foundation for meaningful transformation, we must make the shift from closed to open, from protective to vulnerable.

Vulnerability is the birthplace of innovation, creativity, and change.

—BRENÉ BROWN

AVENGERS ASSEMBLE

Regrets?

I've had a few.

But at the top of my list is a long-standing reluctance to ask for help. Whether I was struggling emotionally or with my workload, or when I could have used input on a vexing business problem, my default was often to go it alone.

In some cases, this was caused by my tendency to be a perfectionist and my need to feel powerful and in control. In other circumstances it was my fear of being vulnerable—to risk being seen as weak, lazy, or unskilled. Often, I erroneously believed I was the only one who felt a certain way, and no one could possibly understand my struggles. In other instances, it was a sense that as a leader, I was supposed to have all the answers.

Regardless of the reasons, it was pretty much always a big mistake. And here again, I was letting my desire to protect my ego rule the roost.

It's not hard to think of the many reasons why it's a good idea to ask for help. Indeed, it often truly does take a village to do anything worthwhile.

But particularly as we focus on building the muscle to drive transformative results, being willing to ask for help is essential.

> ## My mind is like a bad neighborhood. Nobody should go in there alone.
>
> —ANNE LAMOTT

Thinking that one person, no matter how wildly talented, can be the source of enough wisdom to deal with all that an organization must accomplish is the pinnacle of arrogance.

But aside from being arrogant, the complexity of what we aim to do requires not only more help but also a great diversity of assistance.

We need input from voices that represent the views of the rich tapestry of our customer base. We need folks of various strengths and perspectives. We need people who don't look like us, or love like us, or think like us. We need people willing to call us out on our nonsense or push back on our terrible ideas.

PUT YOUR MASK ON FIRST

There is a powerful reason that Crush Your Ego is mind leap 1. Without starting from a place of humility, our foundation will be shaky. And we cannot build a house of sustained innovation and transformation without rock-solid first principles.

This mind leap may also be the most difficult because it requires us to take a hard look at ourselves. It asks us to let go of beliefs, habits, and assumptions that no longer serve the journey we are about to embark upon. It demands rigorous honesty and a lot of courage. It insists that we open up in ways we may not have done before and be willing to fail.

That can be terrifying.

It's also our only choice for making progress.

Sit down, be humble.

—KENDRICK LAMAR, "HUMBLE"

QUESTIONS TO HELP YOU CRUSH YOUR EGO

1. Where are you sometimes your own worst enemy? What are some ways to rethink your approach?

2. What are three critical assumptions or hypotheses you hold dear about the long-term strength of your business model (or brand differentiation and relevance) that might be worth challenging?

3. What are three situations where you might accelerate your progress by asking for help? What's keeping you from doing that in the next twenty-four hours?

4. What would adopting a regular practice of beginner's mind look like for you and your organization?

5. Right now, where are you faking it until you make it? What benefits might embracing vulnerability with your team (or your network) possibly unlock?

CHAPTER 4

MIND LEAP 2: WAKE UP

OPEN THE APERTURE. DO THE WORK.
ACCEPT NEW REALITIES.

The future's uncertain, and the end is always near.

—THE DOORS, *ROADHOUSE BLUES*

I HAVE ATTENDED QUITE A LOT OF CONFERENCES over my career. My travels—as both a keynote speaker and as just a regular old attendee—have taken me to six continents and something like twenty different countries. (And I've yet to lose hope that I will get the coveted opening speaking slot at the Antarctica Retail Expo.)

Such events, as you might be familiar with, typically feature executives from high-profile companies, and their talks are generally meant to showcase a successful case study or perhaps summarize a new way to address a common problem or illustrate a new opportunity.

I don't wish to sound like a grouchy old fella, nor do I want to disrespect the conference organizers, but I have found that a disappointingly high percentage of these sessions are mostly useless.

This is not the result of professional jealousy or my being preternaturally gifted. It is—and there really is no nice way to say this—the result of the speaker's ignorance or lack of self-awareness. In my experience, what often gets shared as some sort of revelation is merely the musing of someone who has arrived late to the party. If anything, what it reveals is that they have not been paying attention to what matters for quite some time or have been failing to do the work required to stay on top of relevant trends.

In the months before I began writing this book in earnest, I lost count of the number of times I heard someone put forth what they thought was a keen insight, when really it was something that just about anyone who has been immersed in the necessary work has known for years. Podcasts I listened to, industry articles I read, and corporate leaders I spoke with were all guilty of this. In fact, at least three different times during the past year, I heard senior executives at different companies quote a finding that we used to include in our public investor presentations way back in 2005. Although we may have been on the leading edge in some respects, plenty of other companies had been sharing similar insights.

How is it possible that so many people come across this information so very late? And why does it matter?

When we take too narrow a view or when we fail to do the work that will uncover the insights that will propel our transformation efforts forward, we sharply increase our risk of getting stuck in the zone of irrelevance. Unless we wake up to new realities and accept that we must aim higher, move far faster, and commit to the action that is implied by said realities, we will be in no position to take the leaps we must.

Before the era of digital disruption, a fair amount of igno-rance and a lack of urgency was understandable. Today, it is both inexcusable and dangerous.

COLUMBUS DIDN'T DISCOVER AMERICA

As a kid I was taught that Christopher Columbus discovered America. Of course, that's nonsense.

The reason he didn't discover it is because the landmasses now known as North and South America had been settled by various indigenous cultures and civilizations for thousands of years. It's more accurate to say he invaded it. But that's a topic for a different book.

My point is that acting as if you have discovered something a lot of people have already known about for a long time is not a badge of honor—it's a sign that you have not done your homework. In a world that is moving very fast and is often very hard to make sense of, failing to educate yourself—to "do the reading," as some have put it—is perilous, indeed.

Perhaps you've been fishing in the wrong places. Perhaps you've got the wrong lens on the issue. Perhaps you've bought into false narratives. Perhaps you haven't dug deep enough into the facts. Perhaps, as discussed in the last chapter, your assumptions, habits, or instincts led you astray.

Whatever the reason, you had better wake up before you drive into a ditch.

SLEEPWALKING THROUGH THE REVOLUTION

As we've covered, seismic shifts began rippling through most industries starting around the turn of this century. And as I've previously argued, there is ample evidence that the pace of disruption is only accelerating. And yet, so many organizations are just now—just *now*—sounding the alarm.

At any time during the past twenty years (or more, in some instances) one did not have to be a keen observer of business strategy to notice these powerful forces amassing, gaining strength, and beginning to wreak havoc. You certainly didn't need an advanced degree or to have received any special training. A subscription to a leading business publication might've been nice, but it was far from necessary. You merely had to be paying attention, be willing to dig deeper, and be ready to take action on what you learned. You had to be open to exploring the perimeters of your ignorance.

Maybe you worked at Folgers Coffee, a product launched in 1850 and subsequently acquired by Procter & Gamble, which by the early 1960s grew to be the country's number one coffee brand. Did you not notice that something significant was happening when Starbucks opened its 500th store? Or its 5,000th? How about when they began opening coffee shops right inside grocery stores? Or when they launched products sold in the same aisles you once dominated? P&G eventually paid the price for their somnambulance, selling Folgers in 2008 for about one-tenth of Starbucks's valuation at that time.[1]

Or maybe you worked at Blockbuster, a company valued at a high of $5 billion before Redbox started to claw away market share by offering a more focused version of video rentals. Netflix tweaked the model further by offering DVDs through the mail, before shifting to its now wildly popular, (and hugely valuable) streaming business model. Today, there is one (one!) Blockbuster store that's still operating (in Bend, Oregon, should you find yourself in the neighborhood).

Or maybe you worked in the department store business, which was once responsible for the vast majority of cosmetics sales. Since 2002, Ulta, a cosmetics, fragrance, body, skin care, and hair care specialty retailer, has increased the number of its stores tenfold. Meanwhile, nearly every department store has shuttered numerous locations, and some once-prominent chains are now gone completely. Although Ulta does not sell any of the product categories that make up (pun very much intended) the bulk of revenues for department stores (i.e., apparel, shoes, handbags, home products), Ulta's market value is, as I write this, greater than the top five American department stores *combined*.

To be both fair and clear, it is not always obvious which trends or business models will take hold. Many so-called game-changing technologies prove ultimately to be inconsequential or well before their time. New concepts that some believe will take over the world (think Myspace, Vine, Second Life, Quibi, Clubhouse) often turn out to be big nothing burgers.

But the vast majority of brands that have gone to the business graveyard (Lord & Taylor, Pier 1, Oldsmobile, and many, many more) or that are holding on for dear life were not disrupted overnight or crushed by a pandemic, nor were they legislated out of existence.

At the core of their troubles was the fact that their leaders lacked the fundamental awareness of what was really going on around them and failed to accept the emerging realities that would upend their once-compelling business models. Having not done this work, they were simply unprepared to act until it was too late.

Dancing through life sounds pretty fun until you have to pay the price. If you're trying to win, better be sure you're dancing to the right tune.

I love you, but you are not serious people.

—LOGAN ROY IN *SUCCESSION*

UNRELIABLE NARRATORS

When we make the mind leap to open our eyes deliberately and critically, we also must actively push back against falsehoods and distracting clickbait.

The world is full of unreliable narrators and people promoting unhelpful nonsense. I'm not talking about your loony, conspiracy theory–spouting uncle or your freshman-year college roommate who now lives off the grid.

I'm talking about guys like a much-venerated Silicon Valley venture capitalist who back in 2013 famously said that in the future, all retail stores will die, a statement that now appears to be one of the dumbest predictions of all time.[2] Although e-commerce has continued to grow rapidly since that prediction, sales through physical stores have also grown substantially, and many thousands of new stores continue to be opened. The issue for struggling retailers is not the growth of e-commerce per se: it is their lack of remarkability. Nothing prevents any retailer from launching a compelling online presence, and in fact, many of today's most successful retailers continue to invest in their brick-and-mortar operations in concert with expanding their digital presence.

I'm also talking about a wildly popular TV financial commentator who has his own network show and over two million Twitter (excuse me, X) followers, and yet has such a terrible track record of predictions that he is known for his "reverse Midas touch."[3] The sheer number of his bad calls would be comical if it didn't potentially risk the money of people who listen to them.

And don't even get me started on the veritable factory of dangerous nonsense that spews seemingly nonstop from the forty-fifth president of the United States.

Aside from learning to ignore the wrong voices, we must also be careful to not fall for consensual hallucinations, to borrow speculative fiction writer William Gibson's phrase. Such hallucinations bedevil our world all the time, be it the nonsense of conspiracy theorists that generate ratings for certain media channels or the hype cycle around certain products or technologies that proponents claim are about to literally change everything (Google Glass, 3-D television, the metaverse). Best beware the peak of inflated expectations.[4]

To fight back against the hype, to parse through the nonsense, it's often useful to ask ourselves: *cui bono* (who benefits)? In many (if not most) cases, it's the person (or group of investors) crowing about the latest and greatest soon-to-be failure.

To drive our transformation agenda forward, we must develop a clear, well-informed view that's rooted in reality, not false prophets. Discernment is a skill we must cultivate.

There's a reason why psychics never win the lottery.

Mulder, the truth is out there.
But so are lies.

—FBI SPECIAL AGENT DANA SCULLY, IN *THE X-FILES*

SOME QUESTIONS CAN'T BE
ANSWERED BY GOOGLE

I am, unsurprisingly, a huge fan of research. Customer research, competitive research, interviewing experts. Bring. It. On.

Moreover, creating spreadsheets and spinning through various scenarios can be incredibly useful in pressure-testing key assumptions. Scenario planning, more broadly, allows us to see a wide range of potential outcomes.

Given all the tools and resources quite literally at our fingertips, it's easy to rely heavily on left-brain thinking and methods that are drenched in massive data and rigorous analysis.

At the same time, if we are to understand where we may be falling short in our transformation agenda, as we skate to and beyond the perimeters of our ignorance, we must stimulate our creative juices.

Several years ago, I briefly worked with a global brand that was kicking off an initiative to accelerate its direct-to-consumer efforts. Although its history was rooted in product design and manufacturing, the company already had a large footprint of its own stores and a significant and growing e-commerce presence.

But they had also been doing the work to understand how they might need to transform to respond to (and take advantage of) many of the shifts I've described thus far—particularly, the expanding web of connection, the emergence of mobile-first shopping, and the focus on developing one-to-one consumer relationships. When I first engaged with them, they were just launching what has turned out to be a multiyear journey to remake the company.

At the kickoff session of the strategic leadership team, I set the stage, presenting my take on the forces that were reshaping the landscape and upending the basis of competition. I was followed by nearly a dozen experts from within the company who shared insights from their respective areas. One of the most prominent design firms in the world also weighed in with their take on how customer experiences were evolving globally.

It was like drinking from a fire hose of fantastic and inspiring input. But it didn't stop there.

That next week, the team headed off on an international tour to get a firsthand look at what innovative companies were doing on the ground. Covering multiple countries and major gateway cities, this tour involved seeing how brands (both well-known and small and idiosyncratic) were transforming their customer experience for a new era. Critically, this investigation was not just limited to direct competitors or even those in adjacent product categories. Many case studies were pulled from food and dining, hotels, and other sectors where a particular execution pointed to shifting consumer preferences and innovative ways to respond.

This exercise in opening the aperture, seeking inspiration

from different fields, and challenging conventional wisdom drove their new growth strategy and spawned many new initiatives. It's also driven a new level of success. Despite being a well-established and comparatively mature brand, the company has managed to dramatically grow its direct-to-consumer business, both in e-commerce and through new store formats.

The lesson here is that the company didn't sit around waiting for market forces to wake them up. They made a conscious effort to do it themselves. And that has made all the difference.

SEEK INSIGHT EVERYWHERE

There is a very good chance that the innovation that will lead to your downfall or is the fulcrum you need to supercharge your journey to remarkable already exists in the world.

It may reside in the upstart competitor that is starting to bite at your ankles. It may be practiced by that fast-growing company in a sector adjacent to what you do. Or it may be found in an entirely unrelated field.

It may be across town; on the other side of the country; or in Seoul, São Paulo, or Milan.

It used to be that the source of competitive advantage could be understood by benchmarking ourselves against best-in-class direct competitors. In a world where innovation spread slowly and predictably, that made a lot of sense. Today, our performance is often compared to our customers' last great experience, which, as you know, could've come from anywhere.

It doesn't matter that we sell industrial supplies; why isn't our search function as good as Amazon's? Who cares that we run a physicians' practice; why can't patients check in quickly and easily like they can on Hyatt's mobile app? Maybe we sell lumber; why can't I order ahead and get what I need loaded up in my truck in a drive-through lane, like what Starbucks offers? And so on.

The future is already here;
it's just not evenly distributed.
—WILLIAM GIBSON

It can be hard to imagine these kinds of novel synergies, if, well, you haven't made imagining a priority. Or if you throw in the towel after the first whiff of resistance or failure. Waking up to what is urgently necessary is rarely a happy, straightforward, or linear exercise.

More often than not, it demands a discovery process that may well take us into dangerous territory with plenty of twists and turns. But take this challenging journey we must if we want to create the conditions for success.

It will almost certainly involve a fair amount of trial and error, and it may take drilling some dry wells, as we will discuss further in chapter 8 (Safe Is Risky). And that's okay. Far from indicating your lack of leadership, it may validate it.

Not all those who wander are lost.
—J. R. R. TOLKIEN, *THE FELLOWSHIP OF THE RING*

TURNING PRO

Several years ago, I had a conversation with one of my closest friends wherein I discussed frustrations I was having with my nascent speaking career. He is a very successful keynote speaker, and I was keen to get his advice.

"Your problem," he said, rather too matter-of-factly for my taste, "is you aren't acting professionally."

I was insulted. "What are you talking about?" I then proceeded to describe and defend all the things I'd recently done to try to become a better speaker. He was nonplussed.

"Go read Steven Pressfield and you'll understand what I mean."

So I did. And he was right.

The concept of turning pro, first shared by Pressfield in his iconic book *The War of Art,* and further unpacked in his follow-up *Turning Pro: Tap Your Inner Power and Create Your Life's Work*, is about knowing and honing our craft. It's about doing the hard, often uncomfortable work needed to increase the odds that we accomplish what we set out to do. It's about showing up even when we don't feel like it or when the conditions are far less than ideal. It's about being disciplined, cultivating resilience, and establishing a regular practice.

I write only when inspiration strikes.
Fortunately it strikes every morning
at nine sharp.
—W. SOMERSET MAUGHAM

Turning pro is a choice.

Turning pro is, as Pressfield reminds us, free, but it's not easy.

Then again, you know what's also not easy? Failing to do the work of transformation and having to suffer the consequences.

Let's be frank. The companies that have gone away, or are currently struggling mightily, approached PhD-level problems with grade-school skills. Or they may have possessed the right skills but didn't do the necessary work to glean the insights they needed, craft the solutions that could have saved them, and move forward with programs that constituted leaps, not half measures.

There is no contradiction between adopting the openness of a beginner's mind and the more rigorous discipline of turning pro. In fact, they are very much complementary. Letting go of old ways of thinking to explore new possibilities will be far more rewarding if we have the skills to recognize the value we uncover. Then we must act with alacrity once our path forward becomes more clear.

RADICAL ACCEPTANCE

One of the biggest obstacles to making the changes I needed to—in my personal life as well as professionally—has been my inability to accept some inconvenient truths or stubborn facts. Because of this, I have often avoided confronting difficult situations entirely.

If you are wondering how that all turned out, the answer is: poorly.

Ignoring new realities or pushing back against their existence is like fighting gravity: you will lose every time. And the sooner we accept this the better.

We don't have to be religious to see the wisdom in "The Serenity Prayer":

God, grant me the serenity to accept the things I cannot change, the courage to change the things I can, and the wisdom to know the difference.

What's the return on ignorance? What's the dividend on narrowness of vision?

I can't give a precise answer, but we can readily see that far too many leaders, their teams, and their organizations have paid quite a high price. Or they are about to if they don't change for a new era.

If we are to transform ourselves and the organizations we lead for a more remarkable future, we must be radical in our acceptance of the truth. There is no benefit to lying to ourselves. We must go *through* our discomfort, not around it. We must embrace reality with all its imperfections and find ways to navigate it more effectively.

Making the shift from an insufficiently examined life to one where we are open, curious, and committed to doing the hard work of transformation positions us to aim higher, move faster, and get more comfortable with making the leaps we must.

After all, it's pretty hard to see the future with your eyes closed, much less leap toward it.

QUESTIONS TO HELP YOU WAKE UP

1. Within the last five years or so, what are three major trends you and your team were slow to appreciate the significance of? Why did this happen? Were there any unreliable narrators that led you astray?

2. What percentage of your time and other resources are invested in learning about and exploring nascent or emerging trends or shifts (customer, competitive, technological) that may have significant potential impact beyond a three-year horizon?

3. What sources of data, insights, and counsel are you employing to inform your growth strategies? Are these broad enough, deep enough, and/or diverse enough to provide more expansive perspectives?

4. Do you have a strategic learning plan that has clear goals, defined accountabilities, and adequate resourcing? If not, why?

5. What are the current or emerging areas where you feel inadequate in your knowledge and ability to glean actionable insights? What would it take to meaningfully deepen your capabilities?

CHAPTER 5

MIND LEAP 3: SPECIAL, NOT BIG

IMPROVE YOUR AIM. DISCOVER YOUR PASSIONATE CORE. EDIT TO AMPLIFY.

Great brands don't chase customers.
Customers chase great brands.

—GARY FRIEDMAN, CEO AND CHAIRMAN, RH

A FEW YEARS AGO I GENERATED A CERTAIN amount of notoriety after opining in an article that "physical retail isn't dead. Boring retail is."[1]

In retrospect, rather than "boring," it might have been better to say "unremarkable," "irrelevant," or "meaningless"—or some combination of the three.

At the time, I was intent on challenging the ridiculous but increasingly popular narrative that we were going through a "retail apocalypse," wherein physical stores would go the way of the dodo bird, largely because of the rapid growth of e-commerce.

The reason I was confident in my declaration was that I understood that, by and large, the retailers that were closing stores had failed to reframe and narrow their focus in a world that increasingly demanded that they do so. The era of "massification" was ending for all but the few that had already positioned themselves to have a vast assortment, low prices, and tremendous convenience all at once. The idea that anyone was likely to out-Amazon Amazon or out-Walmart Walmart was becoming increasingly nonsensical.

What the shift in market dynamics demanded was an aggressive move away from a strategy that was a little bit of everything for almost everyone and toward becoming more inspiring and more intensely relevant for a more tightly defined set of customers. Less was indeed becoming more.

I knew from my years in retail that the mass-market strategy of "Stack it high and watch it fly" that had once made brands like Toys"R"Us, Bed Bath & Beyond, Circuit City, and many others household names and the envy of many had hit a wall years earlier. The retail brands gaining traction with consumers were doing so thanks to their greater focus and deep customer resonance. In all but a few instances, more specific was becoming better than exceedingly general.

Across a spectrum of categories, it was a diverse set of brands like Lululemon, Canada Goose, Trader Joe's, Crocs, Tractor Supply Company, and RH (formerly known as Restoration Hardware) that were finding great success by having a far better understanding of who they were for, what they were for, and what story they hoped their customers would spread. Also, they had the confidence to say no to the customers at the peak of the mass-market bell curve and avoid, as the saying goes, spreading their peanut butter too thin.

This is far from a retail-centric phenomenon. As just one example, in a search world overwhelmingly dominated by

Google, DuckDuckGo and Ecosia have carved out meaning-ful positions. They are not trying to be better for everyone. They are, however, trying to be better for a particular set of someones—namely, those who deeply value privacy in their search activity or who want to be environmentally conscious.

Despite these clear trends, too many companies, in every sector, still plan their strategy around the mantra "Bigger is better." The insistence on tradition—on doing things the old way, just because—almost feels religious in a way. This is not where most of us have any chance of winning. In an era of abundant choice, distracted customers, and frictionless access, where the competition has often built tremendous economies of scale and scope, failure to improve your cus-tomer focus and hone your offering dramatically increases the odds of sinking into irrelevance.

The fact is that no customer wants to be thought of as aver-age. Perhaps paradoxically, editing down what we do—and who we aim to do it for—can greatly amplify its impact.

MASS OR MEANING?

As we've covered, the seismic shifts of the past and the esca-lating pace of change make it ever more difficult to command customers' attention and to engage with them in meaningful ways. And even if we do that well, it still isn't easy to win their business, earn their loyalty, and find ways to sustain-ably generate a return on investment.

The reason why the vast majority of organizations must shift away from a mass-oriented strategy is that trying to find the largest viable audience by casting the widest possible net is to play a game that's increasingly difficult to win. Trying to go after everyone can amount to going after no one.

Meaningful connection between companies and customers is increasingly elusive. And so we greatly increase our odds of success not by going wide and shallow, but by narrowing our focus and going deep. By being specific, not vague. By knowing precisely which types of customers we aim to win, grow, keep, and have spread the story of our brand, and knowing how we will engage with them in a way that is powerfully distinctive and builds an emotional connection.

Said differently, we need to find our who, our what, and our why (as Simon Sinek reminds us). If we can't answer very clearly and persuasively who it's for, what it's for, and why customers should choose us over the competition, it's a good sign we have more work to do.

The good news is that leaping from mass appeal to more precisely defined meaning has probably never been easier (though that still doesn't mean it's easy—an important distinction). Until the past decade or so, the vast majority of our customers were anonymous, or we had very little useful information about them. Highly focused strategies were difficult to craft and execute. When we could not cost-effectively reach current and prospective clients on a one-to-one (or mass-customized) basis, there was little point in highly targeted efforts. The tools and techniques needed to glean useful, personalized insights about our customers either did not exist or were prohibitively expensive, so we did not have the foundation to intensify our focus, to dramatically improve our aim, at any scale.

But now we do.

To rise above the rest, it's worth considering how to chase resonance versus reach.

HUMANS, NOT TARGETS

An essential part of intensifying our focus is understanding whom we seek to serve in a deeper and more emotionally connecting way.

Although it's common to refer to our current and prospective customer base as "targets," I propose we get away from that language. This is more than a semantic point. "Target" definitely implies great focus on the seeker's behalf, but it does not reinforce the other skill that is inherent to achieving greater relevance and resonance: empathy. We must understand people as people, not merely consumers, customers, members, and users. This means dialing down our reliance on left-brain, logic-heavy approaches that center on precisely defined strategies, solving "use cases," employing Six Sigma processes, and the like and instead turning up the art, emotion, and storytelling.

Let's face it. No one actually needs a $5 bottle of water, $125 yoga pants, a $500 hotel room, a $2,000 handbag, or a $6,000 sofa. But the brands that succeed in bringing these products and services to market understand (1) who their brand is specifically for, and (2) how to satisfy both their customers' rational and emotional needs in remarkable ways.

Connecting with our customers' wants and desires, not just their functional requirements—discovering the emotional why behind the buy—is essential if we want to convince them that we truly are special. It's how we will find the higher ground we wish to occupy and command, the highly relevant signal we wish to boost, the story that demands to be told.

EDIT TO AMPLIFY

Central to making this mind leap is embracing the idea of editing to amplify, a concept popularized by Nike and its CEO, Mark Parker. This "less is more" strategy entails narrowing the breadth and purchase occasions of the customers we seek so as to boost the signal of the offerings we wish to emphasize. By doing so, we win through subtraction: we eliminate the cruft, shining a light on what really makes our brand special and powerful.

Editing to amplify is not new. In many ways, whether that terminology was used or not, it has been at the heart of what makes for a great specialty store, boutique hotel, line of specialty tools for woodworkers, or any other more curated, go-to-market strategy. Done right, it makes it very clear who our concept is for, and who it is not. What is new and urgent is just *how much* farther toward greater focus and clarity we must travel.

Some of the power of this strategy comes from the paradox of choice concept. Popularized by psychologist Barry Schwartz and also known as choice overload, this is a phenomenon whereby having too many options to choose from can lead to decision-making difficulties and a decrease in overall satisfaction with the chosen option. The benefits of limiting selection have been demonstrated in numerous academic studies over the years.[2] Indeed, more is very often not actually better.

It's more than theoretical, however. Successful "special, not big" strategies have emerged across a spectrum of industries, perhaps mostly notably in the artisanal premium consumer products space, where shops featuring craft beers, gourmet doughnuts, olive oil, and other gastronomical or lifestyle accoutrements have exploded, chipping away at the hegemony of big consumer packaged-goods players.

Even relatively large brands have seen the benefit of honing their focus. Crocs, the footwear company that has tripled its revenue in four years, credited reducing its assortment by 30 to 40 percent with an overall increase in sales and margins. As I write this, their stock price has more than quadrupled in under three years.

Nike has made editing to amplify a center point of both its product innovation and distribution strategy. Its decision to stop selling through several major retailers in 2020 to focus on a subset of its own more targeted retail concepts and e-commerce perfectly captures what editing to amplify looks like in practice.[3] The share of Nike's business that is sold directly has grown from 31.6 percent in 2019 to nearly 44 percent in 2023.

SO TELL ME WHAT YOU WANT, WHAT YOU REALLY, REALLY WANT

A few years ago, during the Q&A section after one of my talks where I had made a big point about the need to develop greater customer insight, an audience member stood up and said, "So I have a very basic question."

"Great," I responded. "Let's hear it."

"How are we supposed to know what our customers want?"

I paused.

I briefly considered giving a fairly technical answer about the trade-offs between qualitative and quantitative consumer research, as well as a riff on emerging customer insight techniques. But then my smart-alecky brain took over.

"I don't know. I suppose you could ask them."

I will admit that it wasn't my best moment handling audience questions. It wasn't a kind or necessary response. But it did get a pretty good laugh. So I had that going for me—which is nice.

It also wasn't true. Sure, sometimes customers can express very particular wants and needs and we can use that information to deliver better solutions.

But often, customers can't imagine what would meet either their rational needs or emotional desires in truly remarkable ways. The original iPod was not a result of a consumer research initiative where customers opined that it would be great to have a digital device that would allow them to carry their entire record collection around with them.

Ask customers what they want, and they'll very likely request more of what they already like—just cheaper, faster, prettier, or with a few more bells and whistles. They're going to ask for a faster horse, not spontaneously help us invent an entirely new mode of transportation.

The other issue is that in so many cases, different people obviously want different things. Unless you are in the business of commissioned art pieces, bespoke suits, or some other industry where deep customization is the standard, it can be nearly impossible to meet so many different expectations. But the narrower our focus, the easier it is to understand, respond, and powerfully resonate with the customers we choose to serve.

PEOPLE LIKE US DO THINGS LIKE THIS

A major aspect of improving the aim of your go-to-market strategy is to define "your people" and find your tribe (to steal, I mean borrow, another concept from Seth Godin).[4]

Again, this pushes us to go beyond traditional notions of product–market fit that we may have been taught in a first-year marketing class. There is a delicate balance that many customers maintain between wanting to belong and wanting to be different. But either way, it all circles back to finding our tribe of kindred spirits—to identifying as a brand or company for a certain sort of person.

Fashion brands may be the easiest example of how this works. In many ways, what (or who) you wear is as good an indicator of who you think you are as a five-hour interview. As such, consumers readily identify with a particular sort of style or a specific designer that they think reflects their unique values. Other people, though, wouldn't be caught dead in the same styles or designer.

We all know Apple people and Android people; Tesla and Prius people; and those who strongly prefer Starbucks, Dunkin', or the independent coffee shop.

There is a certain set of folks who love a Hummer and a whole lot of someones who don't get it at all.

I'll have what she's having.

—ONLOOKER IN THE RESTAURANT SCENE
FROM *WHEN HARRY MET SALLY*

LET'S GIVE 'EM SOMETHING TO TALK ABOUT

The importance of word-of-mouth marketing is hardly new. But it's still worth taking seriously.

We've known for a long time that creating "raving fans" (as Ken Blanchard and Sheldon Bowles espoused) can be powerful. We typically trust learning about a product or service from a friend or colleague more than we do the self-interested marketing campaigns of the brand purveyor. Word of mouth, or other forms of (positive) viral marketing, are far more inexpensive ways to build demand for what we sell. Moreover, strong advocacy for a company's offerings on the part of its clients can take advantage of powerful network effects. A few of the right people singing our praises can be exponentially amplified, particularly if those people have strong social media networks.

Accordingly, "remarkability" is at the heart of one of the most widely accepted business metrics, the net promoter score, or NPS.[5] NPS quantifies the degree to which a brand's "promoters" exceeds its "detractors." In essence, it captures the relative willingness of customers to share the strongly connecting and positive story of a company's brand. This measure of remarkability has been shown to highly correlate to long-term corporate success. Stated simply, (positive) stories that spread, win.

Giving our customers something to talk about is now supported by research as a savvy strategic move, but chances are we've all experienced this firsthand. We've all likely created buzz within our own tribes about a phenomenal new show on Netflix, an amazing restaurant we just discovered, an exceptional experience we've had with a contractor, or some brand-new product we implore all our friends to try.

The value of these personal endorsements can't be over-stated. When real people—not marketers or company reps—insist how special you are, you'll be in an enviable spot.

In his 2008 essay "1,000 True Fans," Kevin Kelly, the founding editor of *Wired*, argues that in the internet age, "creators" can achieve sustainable success by cultivating a dedicated audience of just 1,000 engaged followers.[6] I like to call them the "passionate core." These fans are defined as people who will not only consistently buy the creator's work without hesitation but also spread the word of the person's work to others in their tribes. Critical to cultivating these fans is delivering something intensely relevant to this relatively small audience and fostering close relationships with them.

One thousand is a somewhat arbitrary number and may not suit your corner of the business world. Perhaps it's better to think about who sits at the center of our bull's-eye: Those people who think we are such a great solution that their loyalty is readily cemented without deep discounts. The types of customers who are likely to trust us so much that they will automatically be interested in an upgrade or our latest new product or service. Who are delighted to give us outstanding net promoter scores. Who will, on their own, help us get more customers like them.

Discovering our passionate core is about creating a minimally viable audience rather than spreading ourselves too thin in a likely vain attempt to capture the total addressable market. It's about finding our fans and gaining confidence about who's at the center of our bull's-eye and who is not. It's about creating a foundation and building on it.

NOT QUITE MY TEMPO

As much as we must find our passionate core and, from there, widen our circle of fans to related customer cohorts, we must also be clear about who's not in the circle—who our brand is *not* for.

There are many reasons why some folks should be way outside our circle. It could be that we have the wrong offering, the wrong messaging, the wrong price, or any number of other reasons why we can't meet their needs, be they logical or emotional.

And that's okay. In fact, it can be a real advantage.

When we chase the wrong customers, we chase our own tail. Attracting the wrong customers can mean we have to discount too much to earn a solid return on investment. Attracting the wrong customers may mean we are forced to endure greater product complexity or higher costs to meet their needs. Attracting the wrong customers may mean they never feel connected enough to our mission to spread the story of our brand. Or they spread the story to more of the wrong customers. Or, their expectations unmet, they may spread a story that is harmful to our brand.

It's best to shun the nonbelievers from the start. It's more than okay to fire customers who don't fit within your focus framework (nicely, of course). Stop trying to seduce the promiscuous shopper. They're just not that into you.

When we truly understand who we want to create meaning for, we put ourselves in a far better position to do something intensely relevant and truly memorable. And to have customers deeply appreciate it.

SIMPLY REMARKABLE

One of the virtues of choosing to be special, not big—of editing to amplify—is how it allows you to create a more simple and straightforward business model.

And it is a virtue. Data makes it clear that these sorts of businesses often do better. For instance, for more than a decade the branding firm Siegel+Gale has tracked the performance of brands that have simplicity at their core of their value proposition, and year after year these brands perform significantly better than their peers.[7]

There are many ways to be simple. It could be the clarity of your messaging. It could be a straightforward product or service offering. It could be the user experience. Or it could be how your overall brand position makes it easy to tell if your offering is clearly for me or not.

Take Southwest Airlines. Although they've gotten a lot of attention over the years for their fun culture and cheeky advertising, the secret sauce of their growth from a low-cost regional airline to a powerhouse generating $25 billion in annual revenues with over a dozen international destinations and some 66,000 employees centers on how they decided to focus on simple.

Southwest's customer experience is much more straightforward than the traditional players. There's no first class, no meals, no baggage fees, no complicated boarding process; if you've been on one Southwest flight as a customer, you know exactly what to expect each and every time. Instead of flying many different types and sizes of aircraft, Southwest only flies Boeing 737s. This greatly simplifies the training and rating procedures for flight crews. Having only one type of aircraft also reduces the parts inventory stocking and maintenance procedures. Additionally, by not employing a hub-and-spoke route system, Southwest contains the potential cascading effect of planes and crews getting paralyzed by bad weather in a major region.

At the same time, the company is also an example of why continuing to invest in sustaining innovation is so critical. Despite the underlying strength in its business model, the company's more recent focus on profits over keeping pace with state-of-the-art information systems has led to some high-profile misfires. In the last two weeks of December 2022—not exactly a great time for operational mayhem— the company was forced to cancel almost 16,000 flights because its scheduling software went haywire. It was a very expensive lesson.[8]

Simplicity has also been behind the remarkable performance of Aldi, Lidl, and Trader Joe's, three of the highest-performing grocery chains in the world. Each operates stores that are much smaller than the typical mass grocery stores by focusing on a particular set of customers and a much narrower range of products.

Even as they've expanded into other products and services, Apple continues to thrive on simplicity. Their core computer and smart mobile device product lines come in a narrow range of options. Their sleek, modern packaging conveys the company's value for function and form. Their operating system makes it easy for customers to be up and running in minutes. Apple is remarkable at delivering great complexity of experience through great simplicity of expression.

A perfect counterexample to the virtue of simplicity is

provided by Victor Gruen, an Austrian-American architect who is often referred to as "the father of the modern regional mall." Starting in the 1950s, his ideas hugely influenced the design of shopping centers for decades to come.

He's also associated with the "Gruen Transfer" (or "Gruen Effect"), the term for deliberately designing a layout so that customers easily become confused, disoriented, or over-whelmed. In this state they are more likely to wander and become more susceptible to impulse buying. Today, many of the hundreds of malls around the world that are a product of this way of thinking are almost comically large and nearly impossible to navigate.

Well, as the kids say, ain't nobody got time for that. Hardly anybody who has more convenient options (both online and in brick-and-mortar stores) wishes to subject themselves to Gruen's brilliance. Therefore, it's not terribly surprising that scores of malls are closing, and many are getting radically reconfigured into mixed-use spaces (offices, hotels, dining, residences, and the like).

IS SMALL THE NEW BLACK?

In a world of too many choices, constant distraction, and endless clutter, it often comes down to this: you can pay for attention, or you can earn it.

Shifting to greater focus; choosing our filters; curating products, services, and experiences; and finding those best-fit customers can be a superpower. Rather than assemble a bunch of stuff and hope a bunch of people like it, we can edit against a smaller set of someones and a more clearly honed idea. And then, through clarity of our brand positioning and more focused storytelling, we can amplify the edit to become a compelling signal amid all the noise.

Paradoxically, becoming smaller in spirit often leads to becoming far more profitable and sustainable over the long term. At first it may not seem like following this approach can lead to a large, scalable operation, but that's not the case. Indeed, there are plenty of upstart organizations whose far more intense focus than legacy-sector leaders has enabled them to leapfrog over their rivals and become very substantial, highly valuable brands.

For a very long time, the prestige cosmetics business (essentially, those brands you can't buy at a drug or grocery store) was dominated by department stores. Over the past two decades, however, Ulta (along with Sephora and smaller players like Bluemercury) has disrupted the status quo through much more focused offerings and their own stand-alone retail locations. Instead of being situated inside a multilevel store in a huge regional mall with a massive parking lot, Ulta's stores are located in neighborhood shopping centers with parking right out front. Instead of presenting products in a sea of beauty counters with brand representatives standing in the aisle ready to pounce on you, Ulta's store designs are open and inviting and mostly designed for self-service.

The result? Ulta now has nearly 1,500 locations in the United States, and its stock has increased dramatically, whereas its department store competition continues to see significant declines.

Or consider Tractor Supply Company, a truly remarkable retailer that focuses on the "life out here" customer. From humble beginnings in 1938 as a mail-order catalog company selling tractor parts, the company grew to open retail stores largely serving farmers, ranchers, and those living in rural communities. Over time, the company expanded its product offerings to serve hobbyist farmers and those with an interest in gardening and livestock. They also began opening stores in smaller cities and on the outskirts of major metropolitan markets.

Their product assortment includes many items unique to their particular style of retailer. But most of the categories they are in (work and recreational clothing, lawn and garden tools, pet supplies, home goods) have plenty of strong regional and national competition, most of whom offer much greater selection and sometimes lower prices.

So how has Tractor Supply Company been able to more than double its stock price in the last three years and set its sights on 3,000 locations? Their strength is in knowing their customers intimately and tailoring what they do to meet their needs more deeply.

At this point, neither Ulta nor Tractor Supply Company can be seen as small in financial terms or store counts. But the clarity of their vision and the tangible and emotional resonance that they bring to life make their passionate, core customers feel that the brand is built for them.

THE POWER OF NO

Drift happens. Once we successfully build our passionate core and carve out a remarkable and profitable market position, it can be tempting to pursue related areas of growth.

Sometimes this can be a wise strategy. In the right environment, leveraging trusted relationships with your most valuable customers to bring new products and services can potentially generate incremental value and help build the proverbial competitive moat.

But just because you can doesn't mean you should. The relentless pursuit of growth may well dilute what makes us special. Saying yes to every seemingly promising new opportunity is one of the quickest ways to pivot away from special to big and unfocused.

Like trying to train a puppy to follow our commands, sometimes we need to be carried back to our center and told "No. Stay. Stay. Stay."

QUESTIONS TO HELP YOU BECOME SPECIAL, NOT BIG

1. To what extent are you targeting the largest possible market or chasing promiscuous shoppers at the expense of a smaller but more devoted segment?

2. How would you describe your "1,000 true fans" or passionate core? Or, if they don't yet exist, what steps do you need take to create them?

3. What are the rational needs and emotional wants you can uniquely deliver to win, grow, retain, and drive remarkability among these customers?

4. Are you satisfied with the level of insight you have about your most passionate customers? What would it take to find and engage with others just like them?

5. What would an "edit to amplify" strategy look like for your organization? Would it involve narrowing the focus of the customers you serve, improving the aim of your marketing messaging, simplifying your product or service offering, or some combination of those actions?

6. Do you currently track your net promoter score (or some similar methodology to gauge remarkability)? If not, why not?

CHAPTER 6
MIND LEAP 4: START WITH WOW

AIM HIGHER. CONNECT EMOTIONALLY.
CREATE MEMORABLE STORIES THAT SPREAD.

People don't buy products, they buy stories.

—BEN MALOL

THERE IS NOTHING WRONG WITH BEING BETTER. Better than we were last week, last month, last year. Better than the company down the street. Better ranking on Google search results than our most-feared competitor.

But better isn't always the same as good, and it sure can easily fall short of delivering the remarkable customer value we need to win right now and to sustain us well into the future.

Of course, we shouldn't let our journey to remarkable be hamstrung by an endless quest for perfection. Waiting for perfect can hold us back from valuable progress. When it comes to many kinds of tactical decisions, or launching pilot initiatives, going with pretty good right now, rather than waiting for the ideal solution, can accelerate our journey to remarkable—as we'll explore in chapter 9.

And yet, if we are going to win strategically over the long term in this era of nearly infinite choice, in the face of so many ready substitutes—many of which may be less expensive than what we offer—delivering a slightly better version of mediocre, or even being quite good, is simply not going to be good enough. We must aim much, much higher.

THE WAY OF WOW

Hop on the internet, drive around your town, or go to your nearest shopping center in search of a product or service and you will encounter a world of decent, expected, and serviceable, but a paucity of powerful, a shortage of surprising. My guess is that most of the options you explored over the last week fell well below memorable. If you talked about an experience, it's more likely it was because of how disappointing it was.

This topic is top of mind as I write this section, seated aboard my umpteenth flight in the past year, on an airline upon which I have flown well over two million miles and sit in the top tier of their frequent flyer program. Despite my status, I can't remember the last wow experience I had flying with them. Do I feel loyal? No. Mostly, I feel trapped.

Precisely defining *wow* may prove a bit elusive, but we certainly know it—and more importantly, feel it—when we experience it. It's the customer service agent who goes way beyond what we've come to expect from a typical call center interaction. It's the impeccable design and service experience from that favorite restaurant where we always go to celebrate special occasions or take an out-of-town guest. It's the feeling we get when we encounter a new store or boutique hotel that seems to have been designed with our favorite touches in mind.

Delivering wow is not about one-offs, gimmicks, or merely garnering attention on social media. We have to go deeper than that by finding one or more aspects of our value proposition to amplify, and using it to create deep meaning for our customers. We have to surprise and delight. We have to create emotional resonance. We often must deliver what Steve Jobs called "insanely great."

I got a fever, and the only prescription is more cowbell!

—CHRISTOPHER WALKEN ON *SATURDAY NIGHT LIVE*

WHY ISN'T BEIGE EVER THE COLOR OF THE YEAR?

Every year, the Pantone Color Institute declares its Color of the Year. In the past decade or so, the winners have included Very Peri, Viva Magenta, Living Coral, Radiant Orchid, Marsala, Tangerine Tango, Mimosa, Chili Pepper, and Honeysuckle. However, if you do a search of the paint colors that actually get purchased the most, you will discover they are all some shade of white, gray, or beige.

If you want to call attention to your redecorating project, get a conversation started, or have your friends tell their friends about your fabulous new living room, you go big, bold, different. But if you don't want your paint choice to stand out, if you want to largely play it safe and merely get the basics right, you choose a color that fades into the background, that is largely indistinguishable from its surroundings.

There are plenty of things in an organization's customer or client experience that should be your beige—the things buyers don't notice because they are basic expectations. But they don't differentiate your brand: they only keep you in the game. People don't talk about these beige qualities much because they only care if they are absent. So, beige alone won't be enough.

If you want to thrive today and in the future, your strategy is going to need a strong pop of color. Or perhaps two or three.

AIM HIGHER

The process of wowing the customer often begins in a low place: customer dissatisfaction. If you can shrewdly address this—turning a "sore point" into a "soar point," as I like to say—you will put yourself in a position to reap the rewards. It may also kick-start your effort to turn the tried-and-true into something noteworthy.

As just one example, Canada Goose, the highly successful luxury performance apparel brand, has introduced "Cold Rooms" in some of its stores. These elaborate dressing rooms simulate harsh cold-weather conditions to allow customers to immediately experience the impressive functionality of Canada Goose products. These experiences are obviously great for the 'gram, but they also dial up the wow by providing a distinctive, intensely relevant means for customers to understand the product's value (and corresponding premium price) in a highly tactile way. It's probably not a surprise that Canada Goose locations with Cold Rooms drive far greater conversion and a higher average ticket than stores without them.

Another powerful example is the iPod. Before its invention, music fans who wanted to listen to their own music on the go had the choice of either lugging overstuffed CD binders around or using an expensive, clunky, low-memory first-gen mp3 player, most of which couldn't hold more than a handful of albums. In one fell swoop, Apple solved this problem, creating a sleek, easy-to-use player with massive storage. Not only was the innovation a wow product, but it also set the stage for Apple to release other handheld devices (iPhone, anyone?) that would propel the company to become one of the most valuable in the world.

Whatever the market or product or service, one of the strategic reasons we start with wow is because we accept that attention is finite. When you wow, you don't have to pay for attention—you earn it.

Paying for attention and then paying again to incentivize purchases is a huge problem endemic to many business categories. As we touched on earlier, brands trapped in the unremarkable middle are often addicted to the drug of endless promotional events—"Super Saturday," "Christmas in July," "Friends and Family night"—and a steady march of discounts, deals, and coupons. Companies that consistently deliver wow experiences for their customers, however, can often accrue enormous strategic value without any of this.

Bed Bath & Beyond, once the leading home goods superstore in North America with peak annual revenue surpassing $12 billion, famously (and, as it turns out, expensively) became overly reliant on its pervasive 20-percent-off coupons to drive its top line; for many shoppers, buying at regular price was a sucker's move. Attempts to wean customers off the discount fix that became the chain's most memorable feature proved woefully unsuccessful. In the spring of 2023, they filed for bankruptcy, and after failing to find a buyer, they ended up closing all their stores just a few months later.

Or consider the insurance wars. Insurance is largely a commodity product, where well-established actuarial science and underwriting practices determine the core economics of a given policy. But to try to persuade customers to choose them and/or pay a premium price, insurance purveyors spend gobs of money on advertising trying to differentiate the largely undifferentiated. So we are inundated with marketing featuring either a gecko, an emu, a humorous psychologist, or some guy in a red sweater named Jake.

To paraphrase one keen observer of this insanity: marketing is the price you pay for making an unremarkable product. There has to be a better way. And there is.

YOUR MEDIOCRITY IS MY OPPORTUNITY

Amazon's founder, Jeff Bezos, famously said, "Your margin is my opportunity," suggesting that the driving force behind the company's phenomenally successful strategy was going after categories that exhibited unusually high profits.

That makes for a nice quotation, but it's pretty clear that this philosophy has not guided the company's growth strategy in more recent years. But it was never great wisdom anyway.

There are other factors that determine whether a category is ripe for disruption beyond historical margin performance. If you want to take on Hermès in handbags or

Apple in smartphones because of their crazy-high margins, well, go ahead, knock yourself out. But it won't end well (#thoughtsandprayers).

If we look at sectors that have been revolutionized by disruption and category leaders that have been put in a tailspin or are well down the road to irrelevance, we can see that their decline wasn't simply because their margins were ripe for the picking. Mostly it's because their customer value was average at best.

Indeed, a competitor's mediocrity can become our opportunity. By dissecting evolving customer wants, needs, and emotional desires, and by leveraging new tools and technologies to attack competitors' vulnerabilities, we can find a wow entry point to lean into.

At the same time, we must keep in mind that something that was once a wow factor can morph into a basic customer expectation, or indeed become largely or completely irrelevant. In this era of unrelenting, accelerating change, former advantages can disappear faster than ever before.

THESE GO TO 11

Coco Chanel famously said, "In order to be irreplaceable one must always be different." But as we've covered, to be merely different is not enough. Not anymore. We have to be unique in ways that create deep emotional resonance and boost our signal. We must turn one or more aspects of our value proposition to eleven.

Arguably, the best examples of this are brands with the highest net promoter scores.[1] To earn such high marks, they must provide a foundation of solid benefits but deliver a real wow on one or more dimensions.

There isn't anything especially remarkable about online shoe merchant Zappos's product assortment, distribution strategy, or marketing. Where they create their wow is on customer service. Unlike most call centers, Zappos's phone reps aren't measured by typical call center metrics like lowering call duration; instead, they are measured by call quality. In one legendary instance, a Zappos customer service rep had a conversation with a caller about living in the Las Vegas area that clocked in at ten hours and twenty-nine minutes (note: the caller did reportedly end up purchasing some Ugg boots).

Optical retailer Warby Parker has completely reimagined the eyewear purchase experience over the past decade, stealing market share from the chains that have dominated the space for a long, long time. First they introduced a home try-on option where they mail you five frames you've selected online, saving you a trip to the store. Once you make your selection, you simply send the samples back in a postage-paid box; this has since been enhanced with a virtual try-on option. More recently, Warby has leveraged their tremendous online success to open some 250 beautifully designed brick-and-mortar locations (with plans to grow to 900 or more), creating a remarkable marriage between digital and physical.

PEOPLE BUY THE STORY
BEFORE THEY BUY THE PRODUCT

I will never say that product or quality is unimportant. We're not going to get very far with a demonstrably shoddy offering. Features and benefits matter. But the stories we tell ourselves and spread among our tribes matter more.

As many have said (and studies have confirmed), we buy with emotion but justify with logic.[2] We may think our heads determine our behavior, but as in so many other domains of life, our hearts are in the driver's seat.

This is not to say that there are not tangible, rational benefits to spending a bit more for greater thread count, pasture-raised eggs, a first-class upgrade, or the computer with the faster processing speed and retina display. But don't kid yourself. Part of your willingness to part with that extra cash is the voice in your head that says, "I'm the sort of person who only buys the best," or "I deserve this." Part of you can't wait to tell others about your cool new purchase or amazing recent experience.

I spent several years on the executive team at what was, at the time, probably the most successful luxury department store chain in the world. Our annual revenues were over $4 billion, and our profitability was outstanding. All this despite being in the business of selling products that no one truly needs.

Day in and day out, we sold shoes, cosmetics, jewelry, and apparel with average prices over ten times the typical prices in the broader industry. Most of our handbags (please don't call them purses) sold for well north of $1,000. If you believe they carry stuff better than the free canvas tote bag you got for contributing to public radio, we sure had you fooled.

Most people can't tell the difference between the $100 bottle of wine from the fancy shop in the hipster neighborhood and the $15 bottle at the chain supermarket. Or that logo on your shoes, shirt, tumbler, or yoga pants. It probably cost the company less than a dollar to manufacture it, and you paid $15 or $50 or $500 extra for the story you get to tell.

And we're glad to do so. Not because we are dupes, but

because the brands that connect on a deeper emotional level deliver remarkable, intangible value far beyond a more prosaic cost–benefit analysis.

OWNING THE REAL ESTATE OF THE MIND

If you've driven on the interstate system in certain American states, you'll be familiar with the many, many billboards for Buc-ee's rest stops. Anchored with a rendering of their goofy beaver mascot, they are plentiful and funny in a corny sort of way ("Buc-ee's: Stopping the pee dance since 1982."; "Buc-ee's: Ice. Beer. Jerky. All 3 Food Groups."). By the time you've driven past a half dozen of them, you're compelled to stop. And unlike many bold advertising campaigns where the invitation is better than the party, the experience pays off when you pull into the parking lot and see row after row of fueling stations, go inside and see an impressive selection of well-presented merchandise and tasty food options, or check out their expansive, gleamingly clean restrooms.

Brands that consistently wow us own a special part of our minds and our hearts—a place that may be influenced by a clever advertising campaign but ultimately rallies around the entirety of the brand experience.

Patagonia's best customers don't buy the company's outerwear or become one of their more than 5 million Instagram followers merely because they are persuaded that the latest fleece jacket keeps them warmer than something they could have picked up for a lot less at Target or T. J. Maxx. The company doesn't drive the top line by offering an endless stream of coupons or bonus loyalty points. Patagonia's best customers are enrolled in the story and promise of the brand.

Not necessarily in a literal sense, like being members of a

loyalty club or frequent buyer program. The more powerful type of enrollment is less behavioral and more emotional, where members of a particular tribe are aligned to go on a journey together.

It's the Harley-Davidson customer who dresses from head to toe in Harley gear and has their brand as a tattoo (i.e., they are literally branded).

It's the "Swifties" who follow Taylor Swift's every move and are whipped into a frenzy trying to get tickets to her shows.

It's the legions of Apple people who line up for hours to secure the latest iPhone release.

It's the fans of Liquid Death, the quizzically named water sold in tallboy cans, who relate to the brand's antiestablishment ethos.

It's any number of logos I could show you that would instantaneously elicit a visceral reaction of attraction, disdain, or indifference.

Wow yourself into your customer's mind, and they just might be yours forever.

UNFORGETTABLE, THAT'S WHAT YOU ARE

There are plenty of times when we just want something serviceable. The week before I started working on this chapter in earnest, I was traveling with one of my adult daughters to the Berkshires in western Massachusetts. We ended up staying in a sub-brand of a major hotel chain. The price was reasonable, the rooms were clean, the bed quite comfy, and I racked up some points in their loyalty program. It was a reasonable and convenient choice in the area where we preferred to stay. I have no strong feelings about our lodging arrangements.

I quickly forgot most of the details of where we stayed and

where we visited. Except, that is, for two places.

The Clark Art Institute, just south of Williams College in Williamstown, Massachusetts, is remarkable in just about every way. The museum campus is vast and features a beautiful array of ponds, hiking trails, and scenic vistas. The building itself, designed by Daniel Perry and updated by Tadao Ando, is visually stunning. The collection is well curated and a bit quirky. Part of what makes it unforgettable is its surprising location, but also its origin story and how all the museum pieces come together in an interesting, unusual pastiche.

The next day we found ourselves wanting some dessert. A quick internet search revealed SoCo Creamery, in Great Barrington, and its stellar ratings encouraged us to make the twenty-minute drive. As expected, the selection of flavors was vast, with some curious options (Marzipan Date Orange Zest, Strawberry Rosemary Shortbread). The homemade ice cream was among the best I've tasted (and I fancy myself a bit of a connoisseur), the service was warm and friendly, and the environment inviting. But what made it truly unforgettable—what took it to eleven—were the interior walls, which were festooned with literally hundreds of cards posted by customers answering the preprinted question: "What do you wish you had the courage to try?"

Some of the answers were hilarious. Many were unique and thought-provoking. Several nearly brought us to tears ("I'd tell my parents how desperately lonely I am all the time."). This wasn't just another place to buy ice cream. It was impossible to be indifferent to the experience.

And you can be sure I'm not the first person to spread the story of this wow-worthy brand.

FINDING YOUR WOW

A lot of companies seem to be engaged in a race to the bottom, caught up in endlessly trying to make what they offer ever cheaper and more convenient. It's exhausting. It is also probably an exercise in futility.

Trying to become the clear and compelling signal amid all the noise, a steady stream of new competitors, and the rising tide of new technologies and ever-shifting customer preferences requires more than most of us have any chance of being able to consistently deliver.

Rather than engaging in a race to the bottom, what about trying to win the race to the top?

Instead of appealing to the lowest common denominator, how about selecting customers outside the masses, ones who will truly value what you do?

What do you say to not only delivering flawlessly, but giving your customers something truly remarkable, something they will talk about?

It turns out that the market for remarkable is never crowded.

To be sure, the gravitational pull to serve the largest possible audience can be powerful. There seems to be a natural force that wants us to regress toward the mean, to do the expected, to serve the peak of the bell curve with the safe and reliable.

We need to resist. We need to fight the obvious, kiss average goodbye, send our condolences to good enough.

That's how you wow. And that's how you win.

QUESTIONS TO HELP YOU START WITH WOW

1. What are the wow dimensions of brands you admire? How about the ones of competitors you fear? What elements can you adapt to your situation?

2. When it comes to your business strategy, which aspects of it are lagging, at parity, or clearly differentiating in comparison to your current and emerging competition?

3. Where are there opportunities to close competitive gaps and, in turn, drive better results (sore points)? What about places where you could lean into your strengths and take your efforts to eleven (soar points)?

CHAPTER 7

MIND LEAP 5: THINK RADICALLY

CHASE UNREASONABLE. REIMAGINE THE FUTURE. RECONFIGURE YOUR BUSINESS.

Destruction after all is a form of creation.

—GRAHAM GREENE, "THE DESTRUCTORS"

VERY CLEARLY REMEMBER ONE OF MY FIRST MEETINGS with Sears's newish CEO, Alan Lacy, shortly after I had been promoted to head up corporate strategy. To refresh, this was shortly before we would launch what would turn out to be a too-timid transformation of the storied and once-remarkable retailer.

As I recall, he started off our meeting saying something like this: "The first thing we all should accept is that in most respects, our current business model makes no sense. If you were starting a retail concept today, there is no way you would create anything that looks like what we do."

It was a harsh statement, to be sure. But it was also true. And what plagued us then was not a situation unique to Sears, to department stores, to other struggling retailers, or to just about any organization that had not reimagined itself for a very different future.

Would anyone build a massive regional shopping mall if they had to do it all over again? Does the idea of an auto dealership on a huge piece of land with millions of dollars in inventory sitting there for weeks on end make any sense in today's context? What about a vast chain of bank branches with many thousands of ATMs and millions of plastic credit cards? How about a massive fleet of gas-guzzling cars cruising around town hoping to come across a potential fare?

How do we avoid repeating the sins of the past? How do we go from being built for an era that no longer exists to one that wins the future?

In this chapter, I offer a bunch of ideas, riffs, and meditations to help inspire you to think more radically, to leap to an entirely new way of doing business.

START WITH WHY NOT

To dream is to risk disappointment. To fail to do so is to risk irrelevance.

We're often encouraged to think outside the box, but maybe we need to forget about the box in the first place?

Sure, there are plenty of failures of execution, as well as misfires in communication that help explain why companies fall short and eventually lose relevance. But in my experience, in so many of these cases, what we are seeing is a failure of imagination. When it comes to transforming at the speed of disruption, it turns out that imagination is far more important than mere knowledge. I'm quite certain the major hotel players know the lodging business pretty darn well, but that didn't prevent Airbnb and Vrbo from capturing most of the incremental value created in the industry during the past decade.

All the vast knowledge and accumulated experience of department store operators, taxi service owners, movie theater chains, publishers of the yellow pages, big-city newspapers, and the three major TV networks didn't seem to help them much during the past twenty years as massive amounts of value migrated to the disruptors that challenged the status quo.

Our starting point can be trying to make what we already do better, or we can start by assessing the ultimate end state the customer is trying to reach and reimagining a novel way to get them there.

Let the old dreams die. We have new ones.
— JOHN AJVIDE LINDQVIST

NEVER IS A LONG TIME

As disruption happens more quickly, reshaping entire sectors, what seemed hard to imagine a few years ago is fast becoming reality.

When I first started outlining this book, hardly anybody was talking about generative AI. By the time I was deep into writing, it was the primary topic of conversation at most industry conferences and was being covered extensively in the mainstream media. Will it live up to the insane hype? Maybe, maybe not. But if you're in an industry that could be majorly disrupted by it, or, alternatively, could potentially exploit it and realize huge gains, it behooves you to pay close attention. To imagine how it might take your business to the next level if you expand your horizons.

What we can scarcely imagine in this moment may well determine our future success or failure. What we once characterized as "never" may well be more like "not quite yet."

THE PERILOUS PROTECTION OF
THE INSTALLED BASE

Say what you will about sunk costs being sunk, but a whole lot of energy goes into defending existing assets, clinging to long-standing customer relationships, and being unwilling to compete with ourselves.

During my tenure at Sears, very promising, new, off-the-mall concepts were either squashed, underinvested in, or slow-walked because we were fearful they would cannibalize our full-line (i.e., large, mostly mall-based) department stores. Sears's once-powerful Kenmore and Craftsman private labels steadily descended from the ranks of the world's most valuable consumer brands (of any kind) mainly because they were not sold where consumers increasingly chose to purchase their major appliances and tools—namely, from home-product category killers like Home Depot, Lowe's, and Best Buy. The various expanded distribution options we evaluated multiple times over many years never went anywhere primarily because we were too worried that selling through other channels might doom our legacy, mall-based business.

Whoops.

The reason that God was able to create the world in seven days is that he didn't have to worry about the installed base.

—ENZO TORRESI, ENTREPRENEUR AND VENTURE CAPITALIST

DISRUPT YOURSELF

Clayton Christensen, the Harvard Business School professor and author of *The Innovator's Dilemma* I referenced in the introduction, believed that companies should be better at competing with themselves than their competitors. He argued that the biggest threat to a company's success was not external competition but rather internal complacency. Companies that are too focused on protecting their existing products and services can miss opportunities to create disruptive innovations that could transition them away from their vulnerable core business to a stronger, more future-proofed position.

Christensen argued that companies should embrace the concept of disruptive innovation by creating new products or services that initially serve small niche markets but have the potential to grow and eventually disrupt the company's existing business. By doing so, companies can avoid being caught off guard by external competitors and stay ahead of the curve.

Said differently, we should focus on disrupting ourselves before someone else does it to us. Pay me now or pay me later, when it's very likely to be a whole lot more expensive, and perhaps impossible.

WILL RERUNS BE OUR HISTORY?

If you are anything like me, much of your success may be tied to repeating some version of what's worked for you in the past.

Just as we tend to go back to the same playbook, we often think that what's made us successful in the past is likely to guarantee continued good fortune in the future. But more and more, that's like practicing driving golf balls and expecting to post a good time running in the Boston Marathon. The game has changed, and so must we.

Although Double Stuf Oreos may be yummy and drive a nice bump in sales, they hardly transform the cookie category. There's nothing wrong with the latest Chai Tea Whatever at Starbucks (except perhaps with the price and the calories), but some new formulation doesn't represent a beverage breakthrough. And yet various product iterations and line extensions are so often what count as an innovation engine across many different sectors.

Returning once again to Christensen's distinction between sustaining versus disruptive innovation, we can see that the importance of sustaining innovation can exist on a continuum. In some situations, delivering comparatively minor iterations of what we've always done on a steady basis suits our competitive situation quite well. Our sustaining innovation programs can, in fact, help fund our short-term needs as we work to build a more successful bridge to the future.

But ultimately it doesn't really matter what we call change. What matters is whether it's enough.

As you've no doubt observed, too many companies rely excessively on the recycling of old ideas. If they had assets that could be leveraged in more profound ways (think back to my example of Sears's Kenmore and Craftsman brands), they let them lie fallow. If we think about brands that have struggled to keep pace with the speed of disruption, it's almost certain that what they thought of as disruptive innovation fell almost entirely into the category of sustaining.

Business as usual is increasingly business as vulnerable.

And what got you here is not likely to get you to where you need to leap. Old keys won't open new doors.

MAYBE YOU'RE ASKING THE WRONG QUESTION(S)?

As we make the shift from assuming the world wants a slightly better version of what we already do to radically rethinking how we go to market, it's worth gaining clarity on just what it is we're solving for. This is an incredibly useful thing to do, especially because we may be making the wrong assumptions about the wrong problems.

Harvard Business School professor Ted Levitt is frequently quoted as saying, "Nobody buys a drill because they want a drill. They buy a drill because they want a hole." That's pithy, but it's also not quite right. Why does someone want a hole? Well, because they want to hang some shelves. Why do they want to hang some shelves? Because they are redecorating their second bedroom. Why are they redecorating that bedroom? Because they are having their first child. And why is it important that this room is outfitted and decorated in this way?

This kind of process of inquiry—often called the "5 Whys"[1]—can help us get at the root cause of the problem we seek to solve and, as a result, position us to deliver more value.

"Design thinking"—sometimes referred to as human-centered or user-centered design—is another approach that remarkable companies like Nike and Apple regularly employ to unlock more comprehensive solutions to problems that go beyond merely tweaking a product's features and benefits.

Here, too, Christensen can be our guide, as he's the originator of the "jobs to be done" theory,[2] which posits that we don't buy a product, we hire a company to do a job for us. When we reframe our thinking to apply this approach, it can allow us to see the actual end state the customer seeks and the ultimate feeling they hope to achieve.

Making this mind leap therefore inspires us to ask more expansive questions. In doing so, it allows us to see a different, more holistic, more game-changing solution.

No worthy problem is solved within the plane of its original conception.

—ALBERT EINSTEIN

BOUNDLESS ENTHUSIASM

Opportunities for organizations to reimagine their futures and execute against them have expanded dramatically as technological and physical boundaries have come down. In the recent past, creating more holistic solutions was hamstrung by an inability to assemble all the pieces, excessively high costs, or staggering complexity. As more products and services can be delivered to customers using digital technology, however, radically new value propositions can be offered.

Until technology costs came down, sharing economy models like Uber and Airbnb were, for all intents and purposes, impossible. Similarly, adding complementary services like buy now, pay later; repair insurance; and the like, to an online product purchase could not be cost effectively executed at significant scale.

Marketplaces operated by third-party entities like Amazon, Alibaba, and Etsy, where individuals or small businesses can sell their products or services directly to customers, have become major components of many industries' ecosystems and continue to grow rapidly. These sites provide a centralized location for buyers to browse and purchase products from multiple sellers while also providing a platform for sellers to list their products and reach a wider customer base.

"Super apps" like WeChat and Alipay are comprehensive mobile applications that integrate multiple services and features into a unified platform, providing users with convenience, efficiency, and a seamless experience across various daily activities, including messaging, social networking, financial services, and more. These apps often leverage partnerships and collaborations with third-party businesses to expand their service offerings.

Many of the traditional gatekeepers have left the building. Many of the roadblocks of old are now gone. As the boundaries have come down, the ability to create powerful new ecosystems, especially on our mobile devices, has gone up dramatically.

BRAND AS PLATFORM

The era of more singularly focused customer value propositions is giving way to operating models built more on the idea of an ecosystem. By this I mean related products and services that are complementary to each other and, taken together, provide a broader set of solutions for a defined set of customers.

Today, many companies are exploring ways to go "beyond trade," as Bain & Company calls offering additional products and services beyond traditional core offerings. This approach is growing so rapidly that the consulting giant estimates that by 2030, more than 50 percent of all retailer profits could come from areas outside of their historical areas of trade.[3]

Apple is often cited as a platform brand because it has built an ecosystem of products and services that work together seamlessly. Customers who buy an iPhone can also purchase apps, music, and other products through the App Store and can use their iPhone to control other Apple devices like an iPad or Apple Watch.

Aggregation sites like Expedia in travel, Cars.com for automobiles, LendingTree for mortgages, and many, many others make it easy for customers to see a wide range of related or complementary options all under one organizing brand. The idea that a brand can go it alone is increasingly anachronistic. Reimagining your brand as a platform to leverage both operational capabilities and loyal customer relationships, on the other hand, can create a whole new range of opportunities.

Another new and rapidly growing area is retail media networks, which allow advertisers to monetize their data to display ads to customers as they shop online or in-store. Media networks are projected to reach over $50 billion in annual high-margin revenues by 2025 in the US alone.[4]

When a brand is considered a platform, it means that it

serves as a foundation for a larger set of products, services, and experiences. That said, the goal of a platform brand isn't just to sell products or services, but to create an entire *customer experience* that extends beyond the point of purchase. Well executed, this can lead to increased loyalty, repeat business, and positive word-of-mouth recommendations.

LET'S GET READY TO BUNDLE

Delivering a bundle of benefits can provide real value for customers and allows the bundler to leverage customer relationships built over time. Conceptually, bundling is hardly new, but most applications of this were, until recently, fairly prosaic (e.g., fast-food combos, cable TV packages).

Disney is a great example of what successful bundling looks like. Its offerings include but aren't limited to the following:

THEME PARKS: Disney operates theme parks around the world, providing visitors with an immersive experience that includes rides, shows, and other attractions (in addition to food and lodging).

MOVIES AND TV SHOWS: Disney is known for its extensive library of movies and TV shows, including those produced by its own studios, such as Pixar, Marvel, and Lucasfilm.

STREAMING SERVICES: Disney operates several streaming services, including Disney+, Hulu, and ESPN+, which provide access to a variety of movies, TV shows, and live sports.

MERCHANDISE AND CONSUMER PRODUCTS: Disney offers a wide range of consumer products, including toys, clothing, and home goods featuring its popular characters and franchises.

The holy grail of platform business models and bundling may be *rundles*, the term Scott Galloway, the NYU professor, author, and podcast host coined for the recurring revenue stream of subscription-based offerings. Customers appreciate the simplicity of "set it and forget it," while companies love the lock-in value these memberships provide.

Quip is a well-known disruptor brand that fits this model. Their electric toothbrushes feature a sleek design, built-in timers, and gentle vibrations to guide users through their brushing. The toothbrushes also come with a subscription service that delivers replacement brush heads, fresh batteries, and toothpaste directly to customers' doors at dentist-recommended intervals, ensuring one never runs out of essential oral-care supplies.

But they are hardly alone. Dollar Shave Club, Harry's, and Billie follow a similar playbook in personal care, as do Hims and Hers for health and wellness, HelloFresh in meal kits, and on and on.

Thinking more radically about the customer value we can deliver empowers us to leap beyond old constraints, like providing a single product offering when a broader solution or more comprehensive service is just what the customer wants.

THE FUTURE IS BIGGER THAN YOU THINK

It may be a bit of an exaggeration to say that our possibilities are endless, that we are playing an infinite game, or that we operate on a plane of pure potentiality, as spiritual guru Deepak Chopra is prone to opine.

And yet it's not the least bit hyperbolic to suggest that your future may exist far beyond the current horizon, well outside the fence you've put around your present ways of operating.

There's a classic story that perfectly illuminates the limitations we can arbitrarily put on ourselves and the rewards from breaking them down. Even if you know it, it's worth revisiting:

> There were three allied soldiers who were fighting in France during World War II when one of them was killed. His friends wanted to bury his body in a special place, not in the field where he had so tragically fallen.
>
> They carried his body to a nearby churchyard that had a cemetery and asked the priest to bury their friend there. The priest asked them if he had been a Catholic. "No," they said, "he was not." The priest said that the consecrated grounds of the church were reserved only for Catholics and therefore he could not be buried there.
>
> Disappointed, the two men decided to do the next best thing they could think of: they buried him just outside the fence of the churchyard.
>
> The next morning, the two friends went back to the church to pay their final respects. When they looked where they thought they had buried their friend, they could not find the simple grave.
>
> Confused, they went to the priest's house and knocked loudly on the door.
>
> "We cannot find the grave of our friend at all!" they said. "We buried him just outside the fence."
>
> "Yes," said the priest, "I could not sleep last night thinking of your friend and the love you have for him. I tossed and turned, until I decided what I had to do. I got up in the night and moved the fence."

Making the shift from conventional to more radical thinking requires that we redefine boundaries, that we fight against our limiting beliefs, that we recognize the lines we have previously told ourselves we cannot cross—and then decide to cross them.

LEAP INTO THE VOID

Voids are empty space, rife with potential.

Sometimes the opportunity to fill a void, to create something radically new, stems from seeing the gap, appreciating what others have missed, and going for it. Other times it emerges from a fearless willingness to explore uncharted territory or remix things in totally new ways.

Gaudí, Picasso, and Pollack; Bird, Miles, and Jimi—they didn't invent their genres, but they went to the edges, defied convention, and took the brave plunge.

Disruption by its very nature introduces something to the world that at some point seemed unworkable or even downright crazy. So, in many ways, thinking radically requires us to engage in what may feel like momentary lapses of reason. But chasing what seems unreasonable is often not only a savvy strategy—over the long term, it may be the only one that has any chance of working.

Don't play what's there; play what's not there.
—MILES DAVIS

BLOW IT UP

As we've seen, the future is increasingly elastic. And so must be our thinking and our actions.

Much of what has been disrupted in recent years wasn't broken. It just was unremarkable, and entrepreneurs were willing to take on the status quo.

Being able to rethink and reconfigure our business model often means becoming unmoored, pushing ourselves way outside of our comfort zone. It also may mean that we are willing to blow up something we don't yet see as defective. That, as the British say, takes stones.

Many of the areas that have been reshaped by disruption during the past two decades weren't fundamentally defective. In many cases they were operating rather smoothly. Taxis weren't broken. There was nothing inherently wrong with Blockbuster's video rental retail format, Borders's bookstores, Kodak's camera business, or Nokia's mobile phone operation. They all got the job done decently.

Until they didn't.

When the writer Graham Greene declared, "Destruction after all is a form of creation," he meant that the process of tearing down or removing something old or outdated can create opportunities for something novel and differentiated to emerge. In other words, destruction can be a catalyst for creative or transformative change.

Greene's idea is a lot like the concept of creative destruction introduced by economist Joseph Schumpeter, who observed that the process of innovation and technological progress can both destroy existing industries and markets and birth new ones.

Blowing up the old to enable the new may seem scary, but there's no reason it has to be framed as a negative experience. What if, instead, you thought of it as a necessary albeit messy component of the creative process?

By embracing destruction as a force for progress, we can break free from old patterns and limitations, opening ourselves up to new possibilities that can help us fight against irrelevance and build a remarkable, sustainable future.

QUESTIONS TO HELP YOU THINK
MORE RADICALLY

1. Where do you currently draw the lines of your business (customers and markets served, distribution channels, pricing strategy, collaboration partners, etc.)? What new opportunities might emerge if you were to remove one or more of those boundaries?

2. What does your competition see that you don't that is allowing them to steal profitable market share from you?

3. If you were to create a new business to attack your company's weaknesses (or mediocrity), what would it look like? Why aren't you doing it now?

4. What percentage of your resources is spent on either protecting your core business or making incremental changes to what you already do? How much are you investing in exploring totally new areas of growth?

5. What boundaries are coming down that have historically limited or made impossible your entry into new areas of business?

6. What initiatives "beyond trade" might make sense for your company over the next few years? What would launching some pilot activities involve?

CHAPTER 8

MIND LEAP 6: SAFE IS RISKY

FIGHT "RESISTANCE." EMBRACE IMPERFECTION. ACT BOLDLY.

Fortune favors the bold.

—VIRGIL

ANY STUDY OF ORGANIZATIONS THAT have struggled, stumbled mightily, or endured a mass extinction event during the past twenty years, will almost certainly show some form of risk miscalculation—often in the extreme. Competitors were underestimated, disruptive technology wasn't taken seriously, shifting customer preferences were dismissed as passing trends, or more likely, there was a mix of all three.

Instead of being afraid that they weren't changing boldly enough or quickly enough, the leaders of many organizations were instead fearful of making a mistake, looking foolish, opening themselves up to criticism, or dealing with any other real or imagined bogeyman. So they took what they saw as the safe and sensible approach: doubling down on what they've always done or pursuing comparatively minor changes—what I recently heard referred to as "infinite incrementalism." Even those who made innovation a focus often subjected anything with the promise of meaningful disruption to excessive study and analysis but relatively little substantive action.

The outcome of this optimization-and-incrementalism approach is that once-iconic brands are disappearing completely or facing greater and seemingly insurmountable challenges. As it turns out, the penalty for inaction can be huge. The ultimate price for "wait and see" or "slow and steady" can be irreversible irrelevance.

The issue at stake is risk—how much of it we are willing to accept.

Accordingly, this next mind leap is a call to reevaluate our relationship to risk. It's not about being reckless or swinging for the fences with every initiative. But becoming disruption-proof does mean accepting that playing it safe and waiting for perfect is in fact the riskiest strategy of all.

This new relationship requires us to acknowledge and confront our fears. We know that fear is a universal language. But as transformational leaders—or people who desire to become them—we must see that it is often our fear that keeps us stuck. It is our fear that can undermine any hope of successful transformation.

FALSE SOLIDITY

There was a time when locking in on a highly specific, rather inflexible long-term strategy was eminently sensible. As leaders, we could more or less flip on the cruise control and wait for the money to roll in.

There was a time when an emphasis on deep analysis,

extensive planning, and highly controlled processes would likely result in the outcomes we desired.

There was a time when we didn't have to tolerate all that much risk, when we could comfortably lean into the conditions that could likely guarantee success—and ignore those that increased our chance of a major misfire.

There was a time when we could avoid adversity rather than accept that we often need to, as my colleague Sterling Hawkins advocates, proactively hunt discomfort.

There was a time, there was a time, there was a time.

Or, to quote Tony Soprano: "'Remember when' is the lowest form of conversation."

The truth is that in our hyperglobalized, hyperdigital business environment, success and failure are rarely far apart.

Just about anything that will really move the dial over the long term—any leap truly worth taking—inherently brings with it a fair amount of risk.

Nothing is truly solid or inherently comfortable anymore. If we are to be successful in this era of constant disruption, we must accept this as our new reality.

THE PAIN OF NOT DOING IT

Show me a company that watched the last twenty years happen to them from the sidelines and I'll show you a company that will be lucky to survive.

In the epic, multiyear battle between Team Transforming for a New Era and Team Defending the Status Quo, we can be pretty sure who will endure. And as leaders, if we've been cheering on the wrong team, it's our own fault if we don't switch sides.

For many organizations, the perceived pain of taking more

risk simply outweighs the pain of doing what has always been done, but perhaps just a little bit better.

Until it doesn't.

And by then, it's often too late.

In an era of constant, accelerating change, by the time you fully experience the pain of your inaction, of your failure to walk through your fears, you—and your organization—may be well past your expiration date.

If we are to create the conditions for thinking bigger, aiming higher, acting boldly, and moving much, much faster, we have to make the consequences of not transforming far more real.

CAPITAL-R RESISTANCE

There are plenty of times when we aren't sure what to do because we haven't done the work. Other times, we've developed a crystal-clear view but decided it's not worth acting upon. That's not what we're exploring in this chapter.

What we will explore are the forces that keep us stuck, that keep us from shifting from a place of timidity and hesitation to one of bold, forward motion.

To make the leap from erring on the side of caution to accepting that our inaction is the riskiest thing we can possibly choose, we have to come face-to-face with the concept of "Resistance."

Author Steven Pressfield's concept of Resistance, which he introduced in his iconic book *The War of Art,* is the idea that there is a universal force that opposes creativity, progress, and growth. Resistance is the internal force that holds us back from achieving what we know we must. It is the voice in our head that tells us we are not good enough, that we don't have the time, the talent, or the resources to pursue our dreams. According to Pressfield, Resistance takes many forms, such as procrastination, self-doubt, fear, distraction, and addiction. It can manifest in our personal and professional lives, preventing us from reaching our full potential in all areas.

Resistance is what keeps companies from trying new things, in general, and from competing with themselves in particular.

Sure, if we do a deep dive into failed transformations or persistent lack of innovation, we will find plenty of errors in judgment, faulty assumptions, underinvestment, and poorly thought out or executed action plans. But we will also find lots of people who knew what needed to be done but simply didn't do it.

Why? It's all about Resistance, which is fueled by fear.

I might be wrong. I might look stupid. I might get ridiculed. I won't get my bonus or that big promotion. I might get fired.

We've all heard that voice that keeps us stuck in a cycle of procrastination. We've all felt the rumblings in our stomach that tell us to slow down, be more careful. We've felt the clutch in our throats that keeps us from forward movement.

The more profound the change stirring
inside us, the more monumental
(and the more diabolical) will be
the Resistance we feel.

—STEVEN PRESSFIELD

The first step to rethinking our relationship to risk and taking the often uncomfortable action we must is to acknowledge that Resistance is real, that we all feel it, and that it will very likely show up when least helpful to making the leaps we must.

In our journey to remarkable transformation, it is most decidedly not about finding the path of least resistance. It is about seeing risk in new ways, accepting that fear is the dragon we must all slay, and learning how to fight through Resistance.

SLAYING THE DRAGON

As it turns out, most human beings are not exactly wired to take risks.

Blame our limbic system. Finely calibrated over several hundred thousand years, it has evolved to keep us safe.

We may not want to admit it—I know I didn't for many years—but as leaders we are typically scared quite a lot. We are often expected to have all the answers when so much of the time we are fighting imposter syndrome. We are counted on to make decisions with incomplete information. We get paid to place big bets on a highly uncertain future.

Fear is real and it is persistent. If we are rigorously honest, it is often the very thing that crushes our progress, that keeps us from taking the risks that can make the difference between leading our teams to remarkable results or keeping them stuck on the road to irrelevance.

If we are to close the transformation gap, then fear is the dragon we must name. Fear is the dragon we must confront. · Fear is the dragon we must slay. As Pressfield reminds us: "Resistance thrives in darkness. Bring Resistance into the light and you defeat it."

It's no coincidence, then, that each of the mind leaps we have discussed thus far involve personal battles with Resistance:

- Letting go of parts of ourselves that no longer serve our goals or the image we wish to maintain (**crushing our ego**)

- Rebooting our mind to be open to new possibilities (**waking up**)

- Forgoing the siren call of incremental revenue from mass-market products to focus on creating something truly special (**aiming to be special, not big**)

- Going beyond good enough or even very good to give customers something memorable to talk about (**starting with wow**)

- Being willing to challenge and possibly destroy what you've built up to reach new frontiers (**thinking radically**)

There will be dragons—big and small—we must slay to conquer our fears and prepare us to leap out of the zone of irrelevance and into the realm of remarkable.

So many dragons. So little time.

EVERYTHING YOU WANT
IS ON THE OTHER SIDE OF FEAR

The evidence is overwhelming, and the verdict is in.

Safe is risky.

In fact, safe is poison, our kryptonite: the eventual under-pinning of our great undoing.

The stuckness you feel as a leader—and the stuckness you experience in your organization—may be exacerbated by weak talent, old information systems, outdated processes, having hired the wrong management consulting firm, or any number of the usual suspects we habitually blame for our lack of progress.

In my own case, before I had my own awakening, I was pretty good at finding excuses. Most were only marginally better than "The dog ate my homework."

This isn't to say I wasn't often successful pushing myself and my teams to innovate or to stretch to achieve important goals. If I hadn't been, you wouldn't be reading this book. But by and large, the organizations and teams I was part of were frequently cowed by Resistance. When I was on the corporate leadership side, I'd frequently argue that we needed more time to roll out a risky but promising new initiative. Or I'd claim that we needed to collect a bit more data, to spin another scenario or two, or to polish our recommendation to perfection. But mostly I was afraid to expose our ideas to scrutiny.

These tendencies continued in my personal life. After I left the corporate world, I procrastinated mightily in launching the blog I had been telling myself I wanted to write and that I felt would be important to propelling my consulting business forward.

I told myself that my ideas might not be good enough.

Besides, I didn't even know what platform I should use! Where was I going to find a creative person to help make the design look better? And should I hire a search engine optimization company?

After many months of hemming and hawing, I asked a writer friend of mine for tips. In essence, he said that none of what was keeping me stuck mattered. What mattered was that I write something, and I publish it.

But, but, but . . .

He pushed back. "What's keeping you from doing that in the next twenty-four hours?'"

Well . . .

It was the jolt I needed to get started. My first piece wasn't great. Nor were the next dozen or so. The good news was that hardly anyone read them. I had no real audience back then.

Even though I have largely shifted to delivering content through podcasts and keynote talks, since that fateful conversation I have written more than a thousand short-form pieces on my blog and as a *Forbes* senior contributor. And now, I've published two books.

Despite having some success slaying the occasional dragon, there have been many, many times when I've known what needed to be done and I just didn't do it. That damn dragon got the best of me. I was imprisoned by worry. And all too often I spent far more time decorating my cage than I did figuring my way out of it.

It may be a bit hyperbolic to say that literally everything we want is on the other side of fear. But if you think you can make the leaps you must without confronting Resistance and slaying that MF-er of a dragon, well, you're kidding yourself.

Fear is our natural reaction to getting closer to the truth.

—PEMA CHÖDRÖN

BRAVING THE WILDERNESS

André Gide is often credited (although apparently erroneously) as having said that "man cannot discover new oceans unless he has the courage to lose sight of the shore," and this has very much been my experience. My most profound growth comes when I allow myself to be physically, mentally, emotionally, and spiritually unmoored.

Sometimes I allow myself to drift somewhat randomly and serendipitously into distant spaces. Sometimes my choices are far more intentional.

Deciding to ask for help when I was struggling involved letting down the facade I had maintained for a long time and being willing to be vulnerable. It was terrifying for me, but had I not done so, I'm convinced I would not have survived. (I mean that quite literally, by the way.)

Opting to let go of my corporate career to start my own business during a global financial meltdown was hardly the path of least resistance. But the more I came to know myself and the direction I wanted to head in, the more it seemed like a risk worth taking.

To be clear, as I touched on earlier, in some parts of my life it took a full-on crisis to compel me to change. Believe me, I wish there had been an easier, softer way. If I had to do it all over again, I'd like to think I could find a less treacherous path.

When it comes to motivation, to waking up, to making a radical commitment to doing what must be done, I refuse to believe there isn't a middle ground between hitting rock bottom and stepping off the pedestal when everything's going just fine. Either way, as it turns out, I got here as fast as I could.

There are many times, however, when we need to boldly move out of our comfort zone into what feels like the wilderness. Sometimes it may seem that we are wandering aimlessly; other times like we are very much in the belly of the beast, seemingly with no way out. If we are steadfast, at some point we will start to feel like pioneers discovering fertile new lands.

If our goal is to stay one step ahead of the customer and several steps ahead of the competition, we need to get comfortable with a fair amount of discomfort.

And you ask, "What if I fall?"
Oh but my darling,
What if you fly?

—ERIN HANSON

WABI-SABI

If you are anything like me, you might be hesitant to share your work with the world until it is polished to perfection. But here's the thing: we can easily wait for perfect for the rest of our lives. And who's the arbiter of perfect, anyway?

Despite its bad rap, imperfection can be harnessed to

positive ends. Indeed, transforming at the speed of disruption requires a willing embrace of it.

Plenty of ancient philosophical and religious traditions have recognized the importance of imperfection and the lessons it can teach. Take wabi-sabi, the Japanese aesthetic concept that values the beauty of impermanence, imperfection, and the incomplete. It emphasizes the natural and simple over the ornate and luxurious, and the beauty found in the flawed, transient, and unrefined. Wabi-sabi is often associated with Zen Buddhism and traditional Japanese tea ceremonies, where the rustic, aged, and irregular aspects of ceramics, pottery, and other objects are celebrated as expressions of the passage of time and the beauty of imperfection.

I don't counsel clients to subscribe to the concept of wabi-sabi for spiritual reasons alone. I urge them to follow it because accepting impermanence implies that they understand that the world is evolving ever more quickly and that what worked last decade, last year, last week, is nowhere close to good enough. When we accept imperfection, it allows us to move more quickly. We accept incompleteness because we understand that prototypes and interim business models are what we need to leap to the next level.

Up and to the right.

And the good news is that there are plenty of customers who don't seek perfection—they seek remarkable.

Be less concerned with the tuning fork and more concerned with the music that moves people.

SHITTY FIRST DRAFTS

Ernest Hemingway said it best, albeit somewhat crudely: "The first draft of anything is shit."

That's a good thing. A feature, not a bug.

As a reasonably prolific writer for the past fifteen years, I've confronted the horror of a blank screen too many times to count. The most important thing when I sit down in front of the computer and come face-to-face with Resistance is to get started. Get something on the page. Don't worry if it's any good. Keep going. The edit and the polish can come later.

Corporate initiatives are obviously more complicated and carry more profound implications than my periodic musings on the future of shopping, how to innovate faster, or what have you, but the metaphor is apt. One of the best ways to break the curse of the timid transformation is to put more unfinished work out into the world.

The simple truth is that you are in an epic battle, whether you realize it or not. You and your organization's reluctance to try more stuff before you think it's ready is what will edge you ever closer to the precipice.

Perfectionism is the voice of the oppressor, the enemy of the people. It will keep you cramped and insane your whole life, and it is the main obstacle between you and a shitty first draft.

—ANNE LAMONT, *BIRD BY BIRD*

SLAM DUNKS AND HAIL MARYS

By its very nature, innovation is risky. So if you want to protect yourself against the worst-case scenario (to the degree possible), your best choice is to take a portfolio approach. Like any program where our results cannot be guaranteed, diversification is our ally. For every set of wildcatting initiatives, we need to be sure we have a few things that are slam dunks—or at least have a lot less risk associated with them. Any program of transformation, particularly more aggressive ones, should carefully understand the potential risks and rewards of its various elements and manage them proactively as best you can.

To be clear, once you've realized that choosing the safe option is often *more* risky, I'm not endorsing recklessness or the embrace of one Hail Mary after the next.

Companies like Amazon and Google that reliably produce a string of innovations employ a diverse, disciplined approach to product offerings that involves risks, big and small. Many of their efforts are bold, and they don't always work. They are comfortable taking said bold efforts because they are also scoring plenty of slam dunks quietly in the background.

In 2014, Amazon announced the Fire Phone as their entry into the smartphone market. Despite much fanfare and considerable marketing, the phone failed to gain significant market traction, and initial sales were disappointing. Amazon eventually dropped the price significantly, but it was not enough to generate much demand. In August 2015, just over a year after its launch, the product was discontinued. The company admitted to having significant unsold inventory and took a write-down of around $170 million related to the device.

This could be viewed as a disaster, but as their former CEO, Jeff Bezos, has said: "We take risks all the time, we talk about failure. We need big failures in order to move the needle. If we don't, we're not swinging enough. You really should be swinging hard, and you will fail, but that's okay."

But companies that are great at innovation aren't all about only doing things at the extremes of the risk continuum. Sometimes their boldness of action mostly involves letting go of the past and venturing into entirely new areas of exploration. Sometimes their boldness of action is ramping up a robust and diverse portfolio of initiatives. Sometimes their boldness of action is being ready to go big once a pilot or minimally viable product shows promise.

It's never all or nothing. But it had better be a bunch of somethings.

Remarkable companies make change for a living.

QUESTIONS TO HELP YOU EMBRACE (SMART) RISK

1. On a scale of 1 to 10, to what extent do you believe your business must take far bolder action to remain relevant in the future? If you rated yourself a 7 or higher, what are the three most important issues that must be addressed?

2. What are the most persistent causes of your Resistance? How might you slay those dragons? (Try to be as concrete as possible here.)

3. If you are rigorously honest with yourself, would you increase the odds of becoming (or staying) remarkable by taking on more strategic risk?

4. If you said yes, what's keeping you from fully leaning in?

CHAPTER 9

MIND LEAP 7: FASTER, FASTER, GO, GO, GO!

FAIL FAST. BE AGILE. INNOVATE AT THE SPEED OF DISRUPTION.

The problem is, you think you have time.

—CARLOS CASTANEDA, *JOURNEY TO IXTLAN*

DURING MY CORPORATE CAREER AND for the past fifteen years I've been working as a strategic advisor, I've assessed many dozens of innovation projects. They've varied greatly in scope, from new retail formats to new product lines and extensions to acquisitions and joint ventures. In most cases, however, the key criterion for the company I was working for (directly or as a strategic advisor) was the idea's potential "materiality." Time to market was a consideration, but the most important factor was whether the project's financial contribution would be meaningful to our bottom line.

This concern typically led us to take a time-consuming, overly analytical approach to assessments as well as an annoying propensity to refer to our goals in tiresome sports metaphors ("We can't afford to hit singles. We need triples and home runs.").

In a largely analog world, this made sense. Companies needed big, scalable ideas, and they needed to be confident they worked before they plunked down a lot of cash to build that new factory, distribution center, delivery hub, hotel, or store. Back in a different era, innovation unfolded in a more incremental, linear fashion. Slow and steady really could—and did—win the race.

In an increasingly digital world, innovation not only spreads in a more exponential fashion, but it can happen in some cases in mere weeks or months. In so many instances, the rate-determining factors of old are now completely different.

As just one example, Airbnb didn't have to take a decade or more and invest many billions in real estate to become a huge player in the hospitality sector. They employed an asset-light model that did not require major capital expenditures to build out their powerful lodging network.

Tesla didn't become the world's most valuable automotive company by replicating the dealer network of its competitors. Instead, it created a completely different model of product design and facility and inventory management.

Successful e-commerce companies didn't have to wait many years to build hundreds and hundreds of stores before they became meaningful retail brands. A software-centric, digital-first model has allowed for rapid scaling.

An athlete's or an artist's YouTube or TikTok video can redefine the culture in a matter of days or even hours, even if your last name isn't Kardashian or Jenner.

Writers, musicians, and other creators used to have to navigate a massive and largely impenetrable ecosystem of agents, publishers, and physical distribution networks to get their work to market and have any chance of finding an audience. Today, as just one example, an author can leverage inexpensive software to help write and edit her book and then upload it to Kindle Direct Publishing, having it available within days (at a price she sets) on the Amazon platform worldwide. Compared with traditionally published books, the percentage of self- or hybrid-published work was de minimis at the turn of the century—now, it represents a material share of purchased units.

ChatGPT (and other forms of generative artificial intelligence) that were largely unheard of during the latter part of 2022 are already beginning to transform major swaths of the economy. Our understanding of the pace of change required to survive now and into the future has been forever altered.

TIME TO REACH 100M USERS

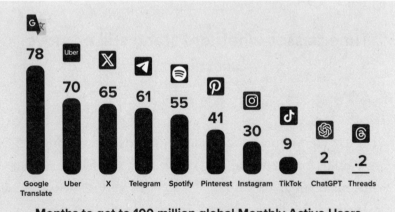

Months to get to 100 million global Monthly Active Users

Google Translate	Uber	X	Telegram	Spotify	Pinterest	Instagram	TikTok	ChatGPT	Threads
78	70	65	61	55	41	30	9	2	.2

Source: UBS / Yahoo Finance

THE FIERCE URGENCY OF NOW

Until the last twenty years or so, most corporate undoings stemmed from slow-motion crises. To the extent organizations found themselves in trouble, their struggles had typically built over an extended period of time. The gap between what customers came to demand of a company and what was delivered unfolded slowly. Tough new competition did not emerge out of nowhere but could be seen coming from afar. As just one example, it took some fifty years for Sears to go from the world's largest retailer to essentially a nonentity.

In the digital era, that is rarely true anymore. Customers share information (good and bad) with their networks about new brands nearly instantaneously. Supply and demand can now be married up with comparatively little investment of time and money to build out vast physical infrastructure. Fast fashion brands can test a new design one day and start shipping it the next. Artificial intelligence allows for the virtual rendering of advertising images that previously took weeks or months to create.

Time passes whether I stand still or move.

—ANN BARNGROVER

If you are waiting to act, exactly what are you waiting for?

Waiting for the world to go back to the way it was? That ain't happening.

Waiting for better data? Competition to become more

rational? Perhaps a sign from above? Well, good luck with that.

Hesitation and timidity are the enemies of progress.

THE CALL IS COMING FROM INSIDE THE HOUSE

Keeping a close eye on direct competition and building the muscle to respond to competitive threats is as basic a leadership tool as one can imagine. Changes in the industry environment, whether due to consumer trends, the state of the larger economy, or new legislation or regulation, must be monitored and aggressively responded to.

To that end, many established organizations typically have departments—customer insights, competitive research, public and government affairs, investor relations—with sizable budgets and outside consultants whose role is to challenge the status quo, evaluate options, or develop specific responses to real and perceived risks emanating from outside the walls of the organization.

These outside influences can be real and powerful. But we should also never underestimate the threats from within.

Very few companies apply the same kind of focused strategies (and manpower) to address the often greater, more intractable risks coming from inside their organization. You might recognize these threats: the defenders of the status quo, the nonbelievers, the constant critics, the passionate bystanders, those who savor the milk of the sacred cows, and those who vocally support any change so long as it doesn't require that they themselves change.

Just as we must personally fight Resistance, we must also tackle The Resistance, the various forces within our culture that get in the way of transforming at the speed of disruption.

ELIMINATING THE DEPARTMENT OF NO

We don't have to be ruthless, but the simple truth is, we can't leap higher and faster when we are weighed down or find ourselves shackled, literally or figuratively.

Transformation is plenty hard enough without people who can't or won't come along for the ride.

Transformation is plenty hard enough without processes and practices that mostly serve as roadblocks.

Transformation is plenty hard enough without a culture that is wired to say no more than it is wired to say yes.

It may not have its own floor in your headquarters or even its own office or dedicated workspace, but most organizations that are slow to innovate have what amounts to a Department of No—or at least a Defenders of the Status Quo club that meets on a regular basis.

Making the mind leap from slow and cautious to innovating at the speed of disruption means getting rid of any drag to your transformation efforts.

This doesn't mean opposing any challenge, pushback, or intense debate. Not only should we be open to these, but we should encourage them. Incorporating diverse and constructively critical perspectives is essential to making better decisions.

But there is a time for exploration, reflection, analysis, and debate. And then there is a time to move.

> There are going to be times when we can't wait for somebody. Now you're either on the bus or off the bus.
>
> —KEN KESEY, QUOTED BY TOM WOLFE
> IN *THE ELECTRIC KOOL-AID ACID TEST*

Let's get real, or let's not play.

The exits are clearly marked. Or at least they should be.

OF COURSE FAILURE IS AN OPTION

Not only is failure very decidedly an option, it is an absolute requirement if you are truly committed to transforming for a better future. Our mission is not to avoid failure; it is, to borrow a turn of phrase from Samuel Beckett, to fail better.

Failing better means accepting that failure is inherent to the process of innovation. To resist failure is to decrease your chance for meaningful success.

Failing better is to rapidly glean insights that will propel innovation further and faster.

Failing better is about failing fast, learning, and iterating quickly to put an even better idea out into the world.

The "useful stumble" offers a perfect example of how this process can work. The term refers to a mistake or an unexpected obstacle that, despite its negative connotation, ultimately leads to a positive outcome or discovery. It's often used in the context of innovation or problem-solving, where unexpected challenges or mistakes can lead to new insights, opportunities, or solutions that would not have been possible otherwise.

In this sense, a useful stumble can be seen as a valuable learning experience that helps individuals or organizations to grow and improve. Rather than being discouraged by setbacks, a useful stumble encourages people to embrace the unexpected and to view obstacles as opportunities for growth and development. By being open to the possibilities that emerge from mistakes, individuals and organizations can find new and creative ways to approach challenges and achieve their goals.

We can beat ourselves up about these perceived missteps, or we can realize that it is impossible to see beyond the horizon without them. A good stumble today can lead to a profound and faster leap tomorrow.

INVENTION IS OVERRATED

We often confuse invention with innovation. A novel version of a product or process can be extremely important, but new ideas in and of themselves rarely determine commercial success. There are many critical steps between the creation of something and what has to happen to deliver and sustain customer value.

In my experience, too many companies approach innovation with the goal that they need a lot more new ideas, when what they need most is to figure out how to speed up the time to market with those that might work. This *may* mean starting with a broader set of inventions. But mostly it means learning to discern the promising ideas from the less robust, refining them quickly, and, again, accelerating time to market.

It is pointless to generate more ideas if most of them won't get in front of customers until it's too late.

QUITTING IS UNDERRATED

There is this idea that quitting is for losers.

But transformational leaders don't buy into hustle porn. The question isn't whether quitting is good or bad. The question is *why* we choose to quit.

If we quit simply because it's too hard or because of Resistance, we may well be quitting for bad reasons. If we quit because we are playing a losing hand or because it frees us up to do more important things, then quitting can supercharge our efforts to move faster in our transformation agenda. In that case, quitting is for winners.

I have worked at and with companies that consistently kept projects alive that held very little promise. That was bad enough. But in a resource-constrained environment, it prevented them from working on far more important initiatives.

Opportunity costs are real. Failure to understand them and act on them is guaranteed to slow us down.

Surrender does not always follow defeat.

The power of no—or no longer—can create the power of now.

DON'T LET SUNK COSTS SINK YOU

A sunk cost is one that has already been incurred and cannot be recovered. It has already been paid and cannot be undone. And yet, many leaders, including those who should know better, still obsess over sunk costs when making decisions.

This phenomenon is known as the sunk cost fallacy.[1] The harmful result is that employees continue to invest time, money, or resources into a project simply because they have already invested a significant amount, regardless of whether the initiative is viable or valuable to the company's strategy.

Essentially, it becomes a zombie project, stumbling around aimlessly and sucking up people's attention that should be directed elsewhere.

In a way, this behavior makes sense. The psychological pain of moving on really can seem unbearable if you've devoted months or even years to something.

Nobody said transformation would be painless, though. Far, far from it.

Simply stated, sunk costs are irrelevant to future decision-making. Just as failure to quit can hold us back and slow us down, so, too, can our failure to properly consider sunk costs in our innovation process decision-making.

SHRINK THE CHANGE

If we are going to truly and rapidly transform our organization for a more remarkable future, suffice it to say that we will be making some rather sizable changes. The prospect of doing this, though, can understandably feel intimidating. Very intimidating.

When confronted with big and hairy challenges, it's often hard to know when and how to start or where to focus our efforts. This can lead to procrastination or dangerously slow progress. This sense of overwhelm is one of the root causes of a too-timid transformation.

If this seems to be your experience, consider the advice of Chip and Dan Heath, authors and experts on behavioral change and motivation. They have written extensively about the concept of "shrinking the change" and its power to help people overcome inertia and more quickly achieve their goals.

In their book *Switch: How to Change Things When Change*

Is Hard, the Heath brothers argue that undertaking smaller changes first can be a powerful way to build momentum and achieve more powerful improvements over time. By breaking down larger goals into more manageable steps, people can make progress toward their goals and build the confidence and motivation they need to keep going.

For purposes of accelerating innovation, this lines up with the familiar ideas of minimally viable products and rapid prototyping. We don't have to have all the steps in the journey to remarkable results sorted out from the very outset. But we can compress the journey over the long run by taking smaller, simpler steps more quickly.

To offer a contemporary example, OpenAI, Bard, and other emerging generative artificial intelligence technologies have clear, immediate applications as well as an intimidating, almost unimaginable range of potential use cases. Given the potentially profound impact the tools may have on so many areas of society and business, it seems like a good idea to experiment with them right now to familiarize yourself with how they work and better understand their range of potential uses.

In *Bird by Bird*, Anne Lamott's fantastic, perennially bestselling book on writing and the creative process, she shares the story of how her brother was struggling to write a report on birds that he had to complete by the next day. Lamott's father told him, "Just take it bird by bird, buddy. Just read what you have in front of you, take it one step at a time, and you'll get through it."

The truth is, there are more mountains behind that first mountain. And our view of what lies ahead will become clearer once we ascend to the first peak. We don't have to have all the answers right now. But we need to move forward. One (brisk) step at a time.

A.B.T.: ALWAYS. BE. TESTING.

Organizations that innovate at the speed of disruption don't possess magical powers or the gift of prophecy. They just try more stuff.

They are constantly testing and learning.

It turns out that reps matter.

As leaders, if we want to accelerate our transformational journey, we need to foster a culture of experimentation. We must, as I implore in *Remarkable Retail,* "unleash the demos."

Much like musical artists create rough initial takes of songs, and painters make pencil sketches to envision their final pieces of work, companies engaged in a serious transformation agenda need to constantly test their process improvements, new products, new services, and other strategic initiatives. The journey that points up and to the right is, at its core, iterative. The more we practice and refine our test-and-learn skills, the better the outputs are likely to be.

As much as we must ultimately strive for remarkable, there is incredible power in *good enough for right now.* This means we must encourage our teams to put more unpolished work out into the world. After all, if you already knew exactly what remarkable looked like, you'd probably be remarkable already.

The path to remarkable is not through extensive study and analysis to try to find the perfect answer. The path to remarkable is through iteration, through trial and error, through taking chances. Through leaps, big and small.

It's through more tests, more pilots, more prototypes—all

with a clear gating process that makes it clear whether we should stop, refine and relaunch, pivot, or step on the gas toward scaling and commercialization.

AGILITY IS THE NEW ACCELERANT

The future is increasingly hard to predict. More and more we live in a VUCA world: volatile, uncertain, complex, and ambiguous.

As the pandemic made abundantly clear, businesses anchored in rigid operating models often struggled mightily to respond to evolving, fluid, and uncertain market conditions.

For years, a highly structured, just-in-time supply chain provided a reliable source of products. Until it didn't. Managing a workforce that went to an office or factory every morning, five days a week, week in and week out, gave managers a sense of comfort and control. Until folks couldn't—or wouldn't—show up.

Mike Tyson put it best: "Everyone has a plan until they get punched in the mouth."

It's obvious that building infinite flexibility into the ways we operate can create unnecessary risk and excessive costs, but it's also clear that locking in on fixed ways of doing business in an era of disruption (digital and otherwise) may well increase the risk of irrelevance.

In the past, operating models that were honed to precision were seen as a sources of great strength. Today, they can easily become huge barriers to responding to shifting market conditions and moving at the speed of disruption.

That doesn't mean we don't have a plan. It means we build agility into our plan.

BECAUSE IT'S 11:30

Saturday Night Live creator and longtime producer Lorne Michaels famously said, "The show doesn't go on because it's ready. It goes on because it's 11:30."

It sure would be nice if we had more time.

But do we actually need more time, or do we need more courage?

In a world where the pace of disruption continues to increase, do we really think we will get to where we need to by riding the brake? Or would we be better served finding the accelerator?

Change is inevitable. Speed is essential.

Point yourself in the right direction.

Flip the switch to Ludicrous Mode.

Step on the gas.

And go, go, go!

QUESTIONS TO HELP YOU MOVE MUCH FASTER

1. Is your organization fundamentally wired to say no more often than yes?

2. If it's wired to say no more often, what are the underlying reasons for this, and how might they be eliminated?

3. What other barriers are causing unhelpful friction in your innovation process?

4. Has your company embraced a culture of experimentation? If not, why not?

5. What could you stop doing right now that would lead to a meaningful acceleration in innovation progress?

PART 3

LEADERS
LEAP

CHAPTER 10

THE BIG LEAP

The best time to plant a tree was twenty years ago.
The second-best time is now.

—CHINESE PROVERB

I CANNOT BEGIN TO TELL YOU HOW WELL I took my own advice in writing this book. The reason I can't is because I didn't. At least not initially.

Early in 2022, I decided it was time to write a new book, one that would somehow or other take on what organizations get wrong about transformational leadership. It was a topic I had been interested in for a long time and had lots of experience in, albeit primarily in one industry. I believed I could add value to the conversation. But I also knew it would take me into uncharted territory.

I intentionally wanted to challenge myself to break free of being "just" a retail guy; I also wanted to write something more personal, more inspirational, and decidedly less prescriptive. It needed to be about a new way to think, a whole new perspective on a topic that historically gets plenty of attention but is not exactly rich with stories of sustained success.

I didn't choose to move in this direction simply out of a desire for greater professional success; or because I was getting a lot of calls from publishers, colleagues, folks that follow me on social media, or friends imploring me to take this topic on. I hadn't performed a market analysis that provided compelling evidence that I had a slam-dunk bestseller in the making. In fact, as far as I could tell, my approach to this material—my desire to infuse more emotional and spiritual elements into how we think about leadership—was quite uncommon in most business books.

In doing so, I came face-to-face with the realization that what I was embarking on might not work.

Like most leaps worth taking.

On my worst days, I was ready to quit. This might suck. Who am *I* to write this book? What will my friends think? A lot of people aren't going to get this at all. Will I not only fail to achieve traction in this new arena but lose that warm, cozy blanket of success I've worked so hard to build over the past fifteen years?

On my best days, I knew all the stuff I fought through during the depths of my own spiritual crisis and during the challenges I faced working on corporate transformations were important for me to sift through and channel into this work.

Yet Resistance showed up constantly. Trying to avoid the dragon, I defaulted to my trusty tools.

As my focus started to coalesce, I did what I've always done when tackling something relatively big and hairy—be that a speech, a new consulting project, or even my first book. I began working on a rough outline, started jotting down idea fragments and quotations that I liked, and bookmarked numerous articles that I might cite as part of my research. As I immersed myself in the initial drafts, I found myself quickly sinking into a familiar pattern.

The way I would convince the reader that I was right, and that my oh-so-brilliant advice should be heeded, was to go to my comfort zone, calling on the very particular set of skills that had served me quite well over the years. Namely, I would dazzle with a well-structured, finely tuned, highly logical argument; beguile with my keen and comprehensive analysis; and overwhelm with mounds of compelling evidence. I would leave no daylight between the persuasiveness of my recommendations and anyone who might take issue.

Bring it on, haters. I'm more than ready.

Deep down, though, I had my (serious) doubts. Nothing scared me more than giving someone ammunition to channel Jeff Bridges's character in *The Big Lebowski* when he says: "Yeah, well, you know, that's just, like, your opinion, man."

As I got deeper into my process, trying to flesh out in greater detail what ultimately became my seven mind leaps, I started to feel a sense of hypocrisy washing over me. My ego and intellect were very much ruling the roost. I was not being very vulnerable at all. I was pulling far too many punches. I was becoming more closed off, rather than expansive. Excuse me while I overthink this.

Well, isn't it ironic?

Consultant, heal thyself.

As I found myself increasingly stuck, I decided to take a bit of my own advice. I reached out to a few people whose perspectives I value deeply and who are more than willing to call me on my own BS. People who are fabulously gifted at pushing me to get out of my head. My ego suitably crushed, before long I went from being overwhelmed and spinning to picking up speed and approaching escape velocity.

EVERYTHING, EVERYWHERE, ALL AT ONCE

If you see a large transformation gap in front of you, or feel like one is clearly developing, getting started on a bold transformation agenda—making that first big leap—can feel quite scary.

Uncertainty reigns supreme, and no matter how hard you work, that's not likely to change much. Our world is growing ever noisier, ever more volatile, ever more complex. The sheer volume of information we must consider and make sense of continues to expand rapidly. Shifting macroeconomic forces along with the prospects of expanding military conflict and the impact of climate change complicate both short- and long-term planning. And then new technologies like generative AI seem to emerge out of nowhere with the vast potential to reset the playing field yet again.

Two things are true at once: It's never been more important to plan for a remarkable future, while at the same time, it's practically impossible to do so with great precision or confidence. The upside is that this goes for everyone—not just you.

In the Introduction, I promised that I would provide a more contemporary (and, dare I say, practical) take on "The Innovator's Dilemma" first described by Clayton Christensen. Part of my underlying thesis is rooted in the observation that so much has changed since Christensen first articulated his core theories on disruption. Today, customer wants and needs are being reshaped by entirely new forces. Technology has been upending the basis of competition in often unimaginable ways—ways in which Christensen could not have foreseen in 1997, when *The Innovator's Dilemma* was published. The pace of change is now accelerating at such a great rate that failure to aim much higher and move much faster risks extinction, not merely decline.

The transformation gap continues to be a real and growing problem for far too many companies. Perhaps even yours. But by now you surely know this—or perhaps are starting to get the same sinking feeling that swept over me at Sears some twenty years ago.

That said, recognizing the problem is necessary but insufficient. So I hope I have convinced you that it's one thing to become aware of an issue and accept its vital importance, and it's quite another to know where to place your focus and your energy and take bold, decisive, meaningful action. This is where my seven mind leaps provide direction and inspiration.

Although each offers its own argument and logic (and what I hope are distinct and highly impactful direction), they all have one thing in common: They all require—sometimes in ways quite similar, sometimes in ways quite unique—tremendous courage. And maybe just a wee bit of faith.

Crushing your ego and **waking up** demand, we let go of our need to feel all-powerful and in control, be open to new possibilities, and continually push against the perimeters of our ignorance.

Pursuing the bold, strategic potential of being **special, not** big; **starting with wow;** and **thinking radically** requires that we recognize that what has brought us success in the past won't get us to the higher ground that we need to occupy. Also, we may need to completely reconfigure the ways in which we go to market.

Accepting that **safe is risky** forces us to confront our fears, brave the wilderness of uncertainty, and reject the tyranny of perfectionism as we strive to leapfrog ahead of the competition.

The final mind leap—**faster, faster, go, go, go!**—commands us to embrace the need for speed and, relatedly, requires us to break down the barriers that get in the way of radical (i.e., fast and profound) transformation. It also reframes failure not as a sign of weakness but as an accelerant to the progress we are called to make.

HOW TO TRAIN YOUR DRAGON

I struggle every day with Resistance, with fighting the dragon that shows up reliably and often at the most inconvenient times. Yet just because we can spot the sabotaging force of Resistance and (hopefully) keep it mostly at bay doesn't mean we ever truly vanquish it.

Do I wish that dragon would stay in his cave? Not so much anymore. When that persistent bastard shows up, I know I'm probably on the path to something interesting and worthwhile. I know I'm pushing up against my edge, that I'm working on something that really matters.

Doing the work of transformation, putting something remarkable out into the world, requires that we learn to train our dragon, that we learn to dance with our fears. We must start before we're ready. We must let go of our perfectionistic tendencies. We must embrace the uncertainty that comes with any creative process. We must accept that fighting through Resistance is a daily battle.

If you feel safe in the area that you're working in, you're not working in the right area. Always go a little further into the water than you feel you're capable of being in. Go a little bit out of your depth. And when you don't feel that your feet are quite touching the bottom, you're just about in the right place to do something exciting.

—DAVID BOWIE

TRANSFORMATION IS A CONTACT SPORT

Why would we proactively choose to do the hard, uncomfortable work of bold transformation? Why would we jump into the belly of the beast, expose ourselves to potential ridicule, and willingly put ourselves into the path of a hurricane?

The only answer that makes any sense is because the pain of *not* doing it will be even worse.

As I've touched on multiple times throughout this book, we don't have to look very hard to find organizations that mostly watched the last twenty years happen to them and ultimately paid a horrible price. It may be hard to calculate the exact cost of a timid transformation, but there can be no doubt that it is often staggeringly high.

Irrelevance is very expensive, indeed.

Sadly, far too many companies believed they had ample

time to mount a turnaround; or miscalculated how quickly shifts in customer behavior, competitive threats, or technological innovation might bring them to their knees.

Objects in mirror are closer than they appear.

The world doesn't need any more passionate bystanders. You must get out of the stands and into the arena. You're going to get dirty, and you're bound to get bruised. It won't always be pretty. But it sure beats the alternative.

No mud, no lotus.

If you are not in the arena, getting your ass kicked on occasion, I'm not interested in or open to your feedback.

–BRENÉ BROWN

WHAT BETTER TIME THAN NOW?

Most days, it's hard to say whether I'd rather have a time machine or a crystal ball. Sadly, I have neither.

I've spent a lot of time over the years beating myself up about all the things I wish I had done differently in the past, both personally and professionally. Maybe you've done the same. More and more, though, I've found this mostly amounts to a waste of time and can cause a good deal of personal craziness. Instead, I try to direct my limited attention to things I can do now.

Although there can be some useful learning gleaned from dissecting the past, ultimately we need to be grounded in the present and shift our focus to the future and those things that prevent us from taking the leaps we must. With apologies to William Shakespeare, the past needn't always be prologue.

We may wish we had started earlier or done any number of things that would have made the road ahead a lot less challenging.

But we must start where we are. Even if the road ahead is bound to be uncertain and bumpy.

We often act as if more study, analysis, and scenario planning will paint a very clear picture of the future.

The uncomfortable reality is that it won't.

Behind one mountain is another mountain. And another. Our view only becomes clearer as we ascend to new heights and see what gets revealed.

If the path before you is clear, you're probably on someone else's.

—JOSEPH CAMPBELL

We often act as if there will be a time when all the conditions are bound to align to ensure our success. But in a world of constant flux and unrelenting change, this amounts to threading a very tiny and rather specific needle.

We often act as if there are a series of actions we can take, over time, that are guaranteed to get us ready for a highly volatile future. I think you know what they say about our guarantees in life.

This is a good place to call back to one of my favorite quotations, from actor Hugh Laurie: "It's a terrible thing,

I think, in life to wait until you're ready. I have this feeling now that actually no one is ever ready to do anything. There is almost no such thing as ready. There is only now. And you may as well do it now. Generally speaking, now is as good a time as any."

LEAPING ACROSS THE CHASM

I briefly considered calling this book *Leaders Leap First*. But that's not quite right.

Being first can be important. But there are plenty of examples where those who move first crash and burn, for all sorts of reasons. Stories of companies being on the so-called bleeding edge abound.

Often, it's an even sounder strategy to be a fast follower, to wait until more facts are in, to learn from those who ventured out to unexplored territory before us. Being bold, making leaps, is not the same as being reckless.

The challenges ahead of us, the ground we must cover, and indeed, the chasms we must cross will be big, small, and everywhere in between. Crossing them may be urgent and important or not so much. Some will demand leaps into futures quite uncertain, and others will require the careful construction of a bridge.

Being first could be a huge advantage. But it's the willingness to leap when it truly matters that is most important of all.

What is a Leap? . . . First, there is vision. You must have your eyes on a prize, somewhere off in the not too far distance. . . . Second, you have to leap versus just walk or even run to that desired prize.

... Third, leaps often require a running start.....
Fourth, leaping requires that you suspend
judgment. After doing all the analysis, gauging,
and estimating of what it will take to make that
leap, faith and intuition must take over. And fifth,
leaping only moves you forward. It is impossible
to leap backward.... Leaping requires exorbitant
amounts of energy and trust in the unknown—and
it always propels us into new territory.

—NATALIE NIXON, *THE CREATIVITY LEAP*

THE BIG LEAP

Over the years, I've asked many audiences and a quite a few consulting clients: "What did you do during the revolution?" Mostly I get a lot of blank stares. It's hard to know if they are confused or embarrassed. Probably a bit of both.

I ask it because I have come to believe that transforming in an era of unrelenting disruption is revolutionary work. As such, it requires radical leadership.

Looking back today, it's all too easy—depressingly easy— to count the organizations that failed to respond to the tectonic shifts that have gripped the business world over the past few decades. The list of leaders who never missed an opportunity to miss an opportunity is a long one, indeed.

If you have made it this far, I suspect you also endured a too-timid transformation or are at risk of doing so. Or maybe you are worried about getting trapped in the unremarkable middle. The data shared earlier in this book suggests you are hardly alone.

But are you willing to do the work?

You say you want a revolution. Well, we'd love to see your plan.

But mostly we need to see you leap.

Here's the thing—and you may want to take notes on this, because it's been my experience that it is true whenever we try to succeed at virtually any worthwhile but inherently risky endeavor in life: No one really knows what they are doing. And the ones that look like they do are mostly fooling everyone around them, including themselves.

You've never got it down. It's this fluid thing, music. I kind of like that. I wouldn't like to be blasé or think, "Oh you know I know how to do this." In fact I teach a class at the Liverpool Institute High School for Boys—I do a little songwriting class with the students—and nearly always the first thing I go in and say [is], "I don't know how to do this. You would think I do, but it's not one of these things you ever know how to do."[1]

—PAUL MCCARTNEY

As we've covered throughout the book, so many of the messages we hear, the training we get, and the behaviors that get reinforced as we ascend to positions of greater leadership responsibility fight against taking transformative action—the kind of action our increasingly dire and perilous situations so often demand.

The only response—the biggest leap of all—is the one where we let go. Where we reframe our thinking, fight through our fears, and commit to a radically different way of showing up as leaders.

That's a tall order.

But in the battle between remarkable and irrelevance, do we have any other choice?

A NEW BEGINNING

It may be the end of this book, but if you heed my call to action, it can also be the beginning of a remarkably better future for you, your organization, the customers you serve, those you collaborate with, and the communities you operate in.

Whether we largely watched the last twenty years happen to us or are just starting to feel the waves of disruption ripple through our organizations, we need to act.

Boldly.

Decisively.

Up and to the right.

Not tomorrow, but right now.

This is the time.

Summon up all the courage you require.

Get ready to leap.

I can't wait to see you on the other side.

ACKNOWLEDGMENTS

L EADERS LEAP **WAS INITIALLY GOING** to be a rather different book. I'm grateful for those special people in my life who encouraged me to be more vulnerable, take more creative chances, and to keep working to slay that MF-er of a dragon.

My eternal gratitude goes to Seth Godin, my great friend of more than four decades. When we first met as undergraduates at Tufts University, it was far from obvious that we would end up as the best man at each other's respective weddings, much less continue to intersect in each other's lives for so very many years. Seth always shows up when I need him and doesn't seem to get too worked up when I shamelessly "borrow" many of his ideas. He's also incredibly kind and generous. Sitting in his living room way back in 2009, during the depths of my "spiritual crisis," I wondered why he suddenly stood up and walked upstairs. He returned with a CD of Pema Chödrön's *Good Medicine* and an insistence that "this will change your life." He was right.

As is probably obvious, I owe a great deal to Clayton Christensen, whose work I have long admired. *The Innovator's Dilemma* inspired many of the core ideas that are at the center of my writing, speaking, and consulting. Those familiar with Simon Sinek's writing will recognize many of his concepts embedded in my thinking as well. I probably should have referenced him more in the text, but he gets enough attention as it is. The same goes for Brené Brown, whose seminal work on shame, vulnerability, and courageous leadership is revelatory.

All of Adam Grant's books are more than worth your time, but *Think Again: The Power of Knowing What You Don't Know* most directly influenced this book. Ditto for Jim Collins's work, but especially *Good to Great: Why Some Companies Make the Leap . . . and Others Don't.*

I have reread (or relistened to) more of Steven Pressfield's work than any other author's, not only because he is a phenomenal writer across several genres but also because his advice on fighting Resistance is so clear, so necessary, and so compellingly urgent.

It's impossible to give appropriate credit to the many other brilliant and inspiring thought leaders who have greatly influenced my view of leadership, but here are a few: Scott Galloway, Rishad Tobaccowalla, Hubert Joly, Tom Peters, Jonah Berger, Daniel Pink, and Ryan Holiday. On the more spiritual side, I keep returning to the work of Anne Lamott, Thich Nhat Hanh, Pema Chödrön, and Jack Kornfield.

Working with consulting and coaching clients, traveling the world to speak, mixing things up on social media, and doing a weekly podcast for more than three years (with my brother from another mother, Michael LeBlanc) allows me to try ideas out in public and engage in (mostly) constructive dialogue. I'm grateful for the challenges, builds, and fact-checks. It's not always easy to hear, but it sharpens the saw. Keep it coming.

Angela Vargo was kind enough to provide wise counsel and dazzling creative input along the way, as well as talk me off the insecurity ledge more than once. John Parolisi, a former Sears colleague, helped me clarify my often-shaky memory while also being a thought partner on the impacts of disruption. And a very grateful shout-out to Dina, Daniel, and the "Tuesday Morning Group."

Special thanks to everyone on the Wonderwell team, including Maggie, Eva, Jenn, J, Liz, Adrian, and Donnie. Extra special thanks to Adam Rosen, my amazing editor, who pulled me back from (most of) my worst instincts and pushed me to lean into my best.

My small but powerful family is a source of support and inspiration that for too many years I did not appreciate as much as they deserved. I am enormously proud of my daughters, Elena and Claire, who show me unconditional love, seem to have forgiven me for my worst moments, and, most importantly, compassionately lend their talents to make the world a better place. My sister, Shari, has always been there for me, in times good and bad. We've grown closer in recent years—most likely because we've both been willing to be more vulnerable.

There are many others, of course, who have contributed to my journey, whether they realize it or not. Any omissions are my fault. Maybe I'll catch you next time.

NOTES

INTRODUCTION

1. I subsequently discovered that my illustration subconsciously borrowed from Clayton Christensen's depiction in *The Innovator's Dilemma* of Product Performance against Time (p. xvi) and also bears a similarity to Martec's Law, also known as the "Law of Technology and Marketing," which was coined by Scott Brinker, the editor of the *Chief Marketing Technologist* blog.

2. Laura Furstenthal and Erik Roth, "Innovation—the Launchpad out of the Crisis," September 15, 2021, in *Inside the Strategy Room,* mckinsey.com/capabilities/strategy-and-coporate-finance/our-insights/innovation-the-launchpad-out-of-the-crisis.

3. AlixPartners, 2023 AlixPartners Disruption Index Report, December 2022, disruption.alixpartners.com/.

4. Michael Bucy et al., "Losing from Day One: Why Even Successful Transformations Fall Short," McKinsey & Company, December 7, 2021, mckinsey.com/capabilities/people-and-organizational-performance/our-insights/successful-transformations.

5. Clayton Christensen, *The Innovator's Dilemma: When New Technologies Cause Great Firms to Fail* (Boston: Harvard Business Review Press, 1997), p. 98.

CHAPTER 1

1. Rishad Tobaccowala, *Restoring the Soul of Business: Staying Human in the Age of Data* (Nashville: Harper-Collins Leadership, 2020), p. 186.

2. Adam Grundy, "Internet Crushes Traditional Media: From Print to Digital," United States Census Bureau, June 7, 2022, census.gov/library/stories/2022/06/internet-crushes-traditional-media.html.

3. Simon Kemp, "Digital 2022: Global Overview Report," DataReportal, January 26, 2022, datareportal.com/reports/digital-2022-global-overview-report.

4. Emily A. Vogels, Risa Gelles-Watnick, and Navid Massarat, "Teens, Social Media, and Technology," Pew Research Center, August 10, 2022, pewresearch.org/internet/2022/08/10/teens-social-media-and-technology-2022/.

5. Rokas Beresniovas (@beresniovas), "Updated #Maslow's hierarchy of needs. #WiFi #battery #digital," X, September 1, 2014, twitter.com/beresniovas/status/506457938056458240.

6. Paul Atchley, "You Can't Multitask, So Stop Trying," *Harvard Business Review*, December 21, 2020, https://hbr.org/2010/12/you-cant-multi-task-so-stop-tr.

7. Ally Mintzer, "Paying Attention: The Attention Economy," ed. Pedro de Marcos, *Berkeley Economic*

Review, March 31, 2020, econreview.berkeley.edu/
paying-attention-the-attention-economy/.

8. Business Wire, "Amazon.com Announces Second
   Quarter Results," August 3, 2023, businesswire.
   com/news/home/20230802612401/en/Amazon.
   com-Announces-Second-Quarter-Results.

9. Steve Dennis, "Retail Reality: It's Death
   in the Middle," *Forbes*, December 4, 2017,
   forbes.com/sites/stevendennis/2017/12/04/
   retail-reality-its-death-in-the-middle.

10. Kasey Lobaugh et al., "The Great Retail Bifurcation:
    Why the Retail 'Apocalypse' Is Really a Renaissance,"
    Deloitte Insights, March 14, 2018, deloitte.com/content/
    dam/insights/us/articles/4365_The-great-retail
    bifurcation/DI_The-great-retail-bifurcation.pdf.

11. Seth Godin, seths.blog, https://seths.blog/2022/06/
    push-vs-pull/.

CHAPTER 2

1. Seth Godin, "In Search of a Timid Trapeze Artist,"
   Seth's Blog, February 5, 2012, seths.blog/2012/02/
   in-search-of-a-timid-trapeze-artist/.

2. Mitch Joel's work has greatly informed my thinking
   over the past decade or so. In particular, his 2013 book
   *Ctrl. Alt. Delete: Reboot Your Business. Reboot Your Life.
   Your Future Depends on It.* (New York: Grand Central
   Publishing) influenced this section.

CHAPTER 3

1. Valerie Young, "The 5 Five Types of Impostor Syndrome," Impostor Syndrome Institute, impostorsyndrome.com/articles/5-types-of-impostors/.

2. Kyle Kowalski, "The Ovarian Lottery: A Thought Experiment from Warren Buffett," Sloww, sloww.co/ovarian-lottery/.

CHAPTER 4

1. Abha Bhattarai, "Smucker to Pay $3 Billion for Folgers Coffee," *New York Times*, June 5, 2008, nytimes.com/2008/06/05/business/05folgers.html.

2. Alyson Shontell, "Retail Stores Will Completely Die Says Tech Investor Marc Andreesen," Business Insider, January 31, 2013, businessinsider.com/retail-stores-will-die-says-marc-andreessen-2013-1.

3. "EXCLUSIVE: Jim Cramer Recommended SVB Financial in February, An Example of His 'Reverse Midas Touch,'" Business Insider, March 10, 2023, markets.businessinsider.com/news/etf/exclusive-jim-cramer-recommended-svb-financial-in-february-an-example-of-his-reverse-midas-touch-1032160650.

4. The peak *of inflated expectations* is a term that comes from the Gartner hype cycle, a graphical representation of the life cycle that emerging technologies go through. The peak of inflated expectations represents the point in the cycle where a new technology or concept generates significant excitement, typically for less-than-sound reasons. During this phase, there is a high level of

attention and media coverage, and there may be a rush of investment. However, this peak is typically followed by a sharp decline in enthusiasm and a period of disillusionment as it becomes clear that the optimistic forecast of growth and impact is not materializing.

CHAPTER 5

1. Steve Dennis, "Physical Retail Isn't Dead. Boring Retail Is." *Forbes*, March 19, 2018, forbes.com/sites/stevendennis/ 2018/03/19/physical-retail-is-not-dead-boring-retail- is-understanding-retails-great-bifurcation.

2. S. S. Iyengar and M. R. Lepper, "When Choice Is Demotivating: Can One Desire Too Much of a Good Thing?" *Journal of Personality and Social Psychology, 79, no. 6* (December 2000): 995–1006, doi.org/10.1037/0022-3514.79.6.995.

3. SGB Media, "Nike Touts Payback from Consumer Direct Acceleration Strategy," October 12, 2021, sgbonline.com/nike-touts-payback-from-consumer- direct-acceleration-strategy/.

4. Seth Godin's concept of tribes was outlined in his book *Tribes: We Need You to Lead Us*, published in 2008. Godin explores the idea that human beings have an innate desire to belong to groups or communities, or what he calls *tribes*. Tribes are not necessarily based on traditional factors (like ethnicity or geography) but can often form around shared interests, beliefs, or goals.

5. Net promoter score (NPS) is a widely used metric to assess customer satisfaction, customer loyalty, and the

willingness of customers to advocate on the brand's behalf. It is typically measured through a survey that asks customers to rate (on a scale of 1 to 10) how likely they are to recommend a company's product or services to a friend or colleague. Customers are then classified into three groups: *promoters* (a score of 9 or 10), *passives* (a score of 7 or 8), or *detractors* (a score of 6 or less). NPS is derived by subtracting the percentage of detractors from promoters, yielding a comparative rating and a basis for tracking relative customer advocacy performance over time. NPS was developed by management consultant and author Fred Reichheld, in collaboration with Bain & Company (where he was a partner) and Satmetrix Systems. The concept was first introduced in a December 2003 *Harvard Business Review* article titled "The One Number You Need to Grow" and was also featured in his book *The Ultimate Question: Driving Good Profits and True Growth*, published in 2006.

6. Kevin Kelly, "1,000 True Fans," *The Technium* (blog), March 4, 2008, kk.org/thetechnium/1000-true-fans/.

7. PR Newswire, "As the Pandemic Makes Life More Complex, People Crave Simpler Brands." December 15, 2021, prnewswire.com/news-releases/as-the-pandemic-makes-life-more-complex-people-crave-simpler-brands-301444323.html.

8. Zeynep Tufekci, "The Shameful Open Secret Behind Southwest's Failure," *New York Times*, December 31, 2022, nytimes.com/2022/12/31/opinion/southwest-airlines-computers.html.

CHAPTER 6

1. Ben Goodey, "Highest NPS Scores: Best NPS Scores from Top Companies in 2023," CustomerGauge, customergauge.com/benchmarks/blog/top-highest-nps-scores.

2. Michael Harris, "Neuroscience Confirms We Buy on Emotion & Justify with Logic & Yet We Sell to Mr. Rational and Ignore Mr. Intuitive," CustomerThink, April 2, 2017, customerthink.com/neuroscience-confirms-we-buy-on-emotion-justify-with-logic-yet-we- sell-to-mr-rational-ignore-mr-intuitive/.

CHAPTER 7

1. The "5 Whys" is a problem-solving technique that involves asking "why" multiple times to get to the root cause of a problem or uncover an underlying motivation rather than merely address a symptom.

2. Clayton M. Christensen et al., "Know Your Customers' 'Jobs to Be Done,'" *Harvard Business Review*, September 2016, https://hbr.org/2016/09/know-your-customers-jobs-to-be-done.

3. Marc-André Kamel et al., "The Future of Retail: The Age of Convergence." Bain & Company, December 9, 2022, bain.com/insights/the-future-of-retail-in-the-age-of-convergence/.

4. Arielle Feger, "What You Need to Know about Retail Media in 5 Charts," Insider Intelligence, November 9, 2022, insiderintelligence.com/content/what-you-need-know-about-retail-media-5-charts.

CHAPTER 9

1. The sunk cost fallacy is a cognitive bias that occurs when individuals continue to invest in a decision, project, or any other endeavor based upon time, money, or resources that have already been expended rather than considering the current circumstances and potential future benefits and costs. This is often a result of an emotional attachment rather than rational thinking and an appropriate consideration of opportunity costs.

CHAPTER 10

1. Robin Hilton and Bob Boilen, "A Conversation With Paul McCartney," June 10, 2016, in *All Songs +1*, npr.org/sections/allsongs/2016/06/10/481256944/ all-songs-1-a-conversation-with-paul-mccartney.

SELECTED
BIBLIOGRAPHY AND
ADDITIONAL READING

This bibliography is not a complete record of all the works I've consulted, but the ones shown here helped shape my thinking.

Anderson, Chris. *The Long Tail: Why the Future of Business Is Selling Less of More*. New York: Hyperion, 2006.

Berger, Jonah. *Contagious: Why Things Catch On*. New York: Simon & Schuster, 2013.

Brown, Brené. *Dare to Lead: Brave Work. Tough Conversations. Whole Hearts*. New York: Random House, 2018.

Brown, Brené. *Daring Greatly: How the Courage to Be Vulnerable Transforms the Way We Live, Love, Parent, and Lead*. New York: Avery, 2012.

Brown, Brené. *I Thought It Was Just Me (But It Isn't): Telling the Truth about Perfectionism, Inadequacy, and Power*. New York: Avery, 2008.

Chödrön, Pema. *Fail, Fail Again, Fail Better: Wise Advice for Leaning into the Unknown*. Boulder, CO: Sounds True, 2015.

Christensen, Clayton. *The Innovator's Dilemma: When New*

Technologies Cause Great Firms to Fail. Boston: Harvard Business Review Press, 1997.

Christensen, Clayton. *The Innovator's Solution: Creating and Sustaining Successful Growth*. Boston: Harvard Business Review Press, 2003.

Collins, Jim. *Good to Great: Why Some Companies Make the Leap . . . and Others Don't*. New York: HarperBusiness, 2001.

Diamandis, Peter H., and Steven Kotler. *The Future Is Faster Than You Think: How Converging Technologies Are Disrupting Business, Industries, and Our Lives*. New York: Simon & Schuster, 2020.

Galloway, Scott. *Post-Corona: From Crisis to Opportunity*. New York: Portfolio, 2020.

Godin, Seth. *Purple Cow: Transform Your Business by Being Remarkable*. New York: Portfolio, 2002.

Godin, Seth. *Tribes: We Need You to Lead Us*. New York: Portfolio, 2008.

Godin, Seth. *Leap First: Creating Work That Matters*. Boulder, CO: Sounds True, 2015.

Grant, Adam. *Think Again: The Power of Knowing What You Don't Know*. New York: Viking, 2021.

Hawkins, Sterling. *Hunting Discomfort: How to Get Breakthrough Results in Life and Business No Matter What*. Los Angeles: Wonderwell, 2022.

Heath, Chip, and Dan Heath. *Switch: How to Change Things When Change Is Hard*. New York: Broadway Books, 2010.

Holiday, Ryan. *Ego Is the Enemy*. New York: Portfolio, 2016.

Iyengar, Sheena. *Think Bigger: How to Innovate*. New York: Columbia University Press, 2023.

Joel, Mitch. *Ctrl. Alt. Delete: Reboot Your Business. Reboot Your Life. Your Future Depends on It*. New York: Business Plus, 2013.

Kim, W. Chan, and Renée Mauborgne. *Blue Ocean Strategy: How to Create Uncontested Market Space and Make the Competition Irrelevant*. Boston: Harvard Business Review Press, 2004.

Li, Charlene. *The Disruption Mindset: Why Some Organizations Transform While Others Fail*. Ideapress Publishing, 2019.

Lobaugh, Kasey, Christina Bieniek, Bobby Stephens, and Preeti Pincha. "The Great Retail Bifurcation: Why the Retail 'Apocalypse' Is Really a Renaissance," Deloitte Insights, March 14, 2018, deloitte.com/content/dam/insights/us/arti cles/4365_The-great-retail-bifurcation/DI_The-great-re tail-bifurcation.pdf.

Moore, Geoffrey A. *Crossing the Chasm: Marketing and Selling Disruptive Products to Mainstream Customers*. New York: HarperBusiness, 1991.

Nhat Hanh, Thich. *No Mud, No Lotus: The Art of Transforming Suffering*. Berkeley: Parallax Press, 2014.

Peters, Tom. *The Pursuit of Wow! Every Person's Guide to Topsy-Turvy Times*. New York: Vintage Books, 1994.

Pine II, B. Joseph, and James H. Gilmore. *The Experience Economy: Competing for Customer Time, Attention, and Money* (revised edition). Boston: Harvard Business Review Press, 2019.

Pressfield, Steven. *Do the Work!: Overcome Resistance and Get Out of Your Own Way*. New York: Black Irish Entertainment, 2011.

Pressfield, Steven. *The War of Art: Winning the Inner Creative Battle*. New York: Rugged Land/Simon & Schuster, 2002.

Pressfield, Steven. *Turning Pro: Tap Your Inner Power and Create Your Life's Work*. New York: Black Irish Entertainment, 2012.

Real, Terrence. *I Don't Want to Talk about It: Overcoming the Secret Legacy of Male Depression*. New York: Scribner, 1997.

Sinek, Simon. *Start with Why: How Great Leaders Inspire Everyone to Take Action*. New York: Portfolio, 2009.

Suzuki, Shunryu. *Zen Mind, Beginner's Mind*. Boston: Shambala Publications, 2006.

Tobaccowala, Rishad T. *Restoring the Soul of Business: Staying Human in the Age of Data*. Nashville: HarperCollins Leadership, 2020.

ABOUT THE AUTHOR

STEVE DENNIS is a strategy consultant, board advisor, keynote speaker, and bestselling author focused on transformational leadership and the impact of digital disruption. He has been named a top global retail influencer by more than a dozen organizations, and his ideas on the future of shopping and how to accelerate innovation are regularly featured in the media, in his role as a *Forbes* senior contributor, and through his top-rated *Remarkable Retail* podcast.

Steve is the president of SageBerry Consulting, an advisory firm that has helped dozens of organizations accelerate their journey to remarkable results. Prior to founding SageBerry, he was a senior operating and strategy executive at several Fortune 500 companies.

As a sought-out speaker, Steve has taken the stage at industry conferences and corporate events across six continents.

His first book, *Remarkable Retail: How to Win and Keep Customers in the Age of Disruption,* is one of the most successful retail strategy books of all time.

ABOUT THE AUTHOR

Steve received his MBA from Harvard Business School and a BA in Economics from Tufts University.

To learn more, go to www.stevenpdennis.com, or follow him @stevenpdennis on most social media platforms.

ALSO BY STEVE DENNIS

Completely **UPDATED** for the **POST-COVID ECONOMY**

REMARKABLE

HOW TO WIN & KEEP CUSTOMERS IN THE AGE OF DISRUPTION

RETAIL

STEVE DENNIS

Foreword by **SUCHARITA KODALI**, Forrester retail industry analyst